7
Steps
to successful
Boat Docking

By USCG Licensed Captains Ronald & Katherine Giampietro Redmond

Sea Search School of
Seamanship

712 North Liberty Drive

Tomkins Cove, NY 10986

845.942.7245

www.boatinstruction.com

Illustrations are by the authors

Library of Congress Cataloging-in-Publication Data

Redmond, Ronald & Katherine Giampietro.
    7 Steps to Successful Boat Docking / by
       Ronald & Katherine Giampietro Redmond
          p.   cm.
      ISBN 978-0-9711911-3-6
      1. Boats and boating. 2. Mooring of ships
      I. Title

Printed in the United States of America

INTRODUCTION

Congratulations! You have probably just bought a new vessel, or perhaps it is a previously owned vessel that is new to you, **or** maybe you are one of the estimated 30% of boat owners who *never* leave their slip because they are concerned that they may not be able to bring their vessel back into its slip safely. Or you may even be that someone who spends half of his/her boating ventures worrying about that increasing wind or current that will change the docking process into a gut-wrenching nightmare. Regardless of your personal reasons for reading this book, unless you are one of those lucky dock jocks who were born with a boat tiller or steering wheel in their hands, you will always be plagued by the helm trembles.

We began boating more than thirty years ago. Stuffing the boat with food and kids, Ron learned to muscle the boats successfully through trial and error.

Years later, as the boats and the children grew up, it became apparent that my lower back had also evolved...into a weak point. It was obvious that my life as a line handler was over. I suggested to Ron that he should consider getting himself better crew. After 30 or so years of marriage, he took a *really* long time to think about it, but he finally came up with a solution: I should drive the boat and he would handle the lines!

Thus began a metamorphosis that is the foundation of this book. At first, I was a satellite helmsperson, attached by walkie-talkie to Ron, who attempted to guide his robot by startling shouts into the earphones: *STARBOARD!* **PORT, PORT! HARD REVERSE!** It was a bone-chilling exercise for both of us, and one that was doomed to failure. It just took too much time for his directions to go thru my brain and into my arms. So I had to take a giant deep breath and learn to dock on my own. This book will share with you the lessons we learned.

TABLE OF CONTENTS

TABLE OF CONTENTS

DOCKING VOCABULARY

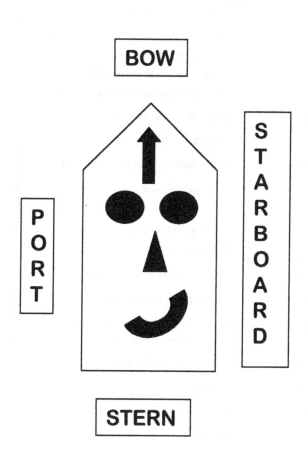

BOW

STARBOARD

PORT

STERN

DOCKING VOCABULARY

To understand the fundamentals of boat docking, you need to know four vocabulary words which are related to all boats:

BOW: the front of the boat, when facing forward

STERN: the back of the boat, when facing forward

PORT: the left side of the boat, when facing forward [memory aid: port has four letters, left has four letters]

STARBOARD: the right side of the boat, when facing forward

MUST KNOW BEFORE YOU GO

VESSELS NEED TO BE MECHANICALLY SOUND BEFORE THEY CAN BE DOCKED SUCCESSFULLY!

As we were hired to train skippers who were struggling with the docking process, it was amazing to find that so many of their vessels were not mechanically sound. The problems ranged from twin engines which were not synchronized, to gear shifts which were erratically responsive. Before you attribute your docking problems to your technique, be sure that your vessel is functioning properly.

DOCK LINES ARE NOT BRAKES!

Some skippers are under the impression that dock lines are used to stop the movement of their vessel. This is erroneous, and could be dangerous. While dock lines play an important role in holding a boat to a pier or in a slip, they should not be used to stop the movement of a vessel. The helmsman's job [the one with the steering wheel or tiller in his/her hands] is to stop the movement of the vessel.

LINE HANDLERS SHOULD "STEP OFF", NOT "JUMP OFF" THE BOAT!

Line handlers are a vital part of successfully docking a vessel. However, the helmsman has an obligation to put the boat in a position where the line handler can step off onto the pier safely. Jumping off boats has caused many a sprained ankle, at the least, and line handlers should not attempt this maneuver. The line handler should be patient, and wait for the vessel to be stopped at a position where they can step off.

MUST KNOW BEFORE YOU GO

DOCKING DOES NOT INVOLVE 8 PEOPLE AND LOTS OF SCREAMING!

While all of us appreciate a helping hand when docking our boats, the helmsman has the obligation to steer the boat into the slip safely. Indeed, with experience, many skippers can "single-hand" their vessel into a slip. Do not get into the habit of depending upon people ashore or you will never develop controlled docking techniques.

Especially when we are new or stressed dockers, we feel embarrassed if our docking technique is less than perfect. However, most individuals are very tolerant of docking mishaps [we all have them]; it is the yelled blaming that provokes ridicule. Make a pact between all parties involved in the docking process:
UNDER NO CIRCUMSTANCES WILL ANYONE YELL OR BLAME THE OTHER PARTY PUBLICLY FOR A REAL OR PERCEIVED ERROR MADE IN THE PROCESS OF BOAT DOCKING.
In the end, you will at least have your dignity!

SIZE MATTERS!

Having docked vessels of all sizes and shapes, it is our opinion that bigger is better. While smaller boats usually provide better visibility of sides and stern of vessel, this advantage is negated by the fact that smaller boats are usually kicked around easier by wind and current than the larger vessels while docking.

MUST KNOW BEFORE YOU GO

START OFF CORRECTLY: CENTER THE STEERING WHEEL!

Many new dockers have been puzzled when their twin inboard-engine vessel does not respond properly to their commands. Too often, this occurs because the steering wheel is not centered. To center the wheel, turn the wheel all the way to the right. Hold the top of the wheel and count the number of full turns of the wheel before it is unable to turn to the left. Divide the number of full turns in half to arrive at the wheel centering position. For example, I can turn the wheel five full turns to the left; therefore, after turning my wheel all the way to the right, I must turn it 2-1/2 turns to the left to center it.

FENDERS ON BOTH SIDES OF VESSEL!

When preparing your vessel for docking, place fenders on BOTH sides of the boat. This is useful, especially with inexperienced skippers, since the extra protection can come in handy in unexpected, close-quarter situations.

LEARN SLOWLY, UNDER CALM CONDITIONS: NO PANIC, NO PRESSURE!

If you decided that you were going to firm up your body and get in shape, you might join a gym or buy some weights and a video and start a gradually escalating program of body building. It would seem ludicrous and dangerous if someone suggested that a neophyte bodybuilder should begin with 150 pound barbells. Yet hundreds of thousands of new boat owners think nothing of taking their vessels out of their slip without bothering to build the muscles of boat docking. Start off slow, in calm conditions, and build skills and confidence.

MUST KNOW BEFORE YOU GO

BEFORE YOU CAN DOCK YOUR BOAT, YOU MUST KNOW HOW IT WILL RESPOND TO YOUR COMMANDS!

A fellow who took our Boat Docking Tips Course said that he was afraid as he entered his slip because he did not know how long it would take for his boat to stop. His fear was understandable. Can you imagine your fear every time you approached a stoplight if you did not know how far your car would travel after you stepped on the brake?

Before you can safely and confidently dock your boat, you must know how your boat will react to your commands, keeping in mind that conditions will alter those reactions a little or a lot, depending upon external forces. That is why this book includes Skill Drills, which are the muscle builders of boat docking. Those drills dissect docking into digestible bits that will reinforce the basic boat movements you need to know before you slide your vessel into its slip. [Skill Drills are listed in the back of the docking sections for each specific type of vessel.]

How long will it take for my boat to stop when I engage forward gear and use reverse to stop?

What maneuvers must I use to hold my boat in place?

How far will momentum take my vessel when I engage forward gear, then go immediately to neutral?

How sharply will my vessel turn when I move the wheel hard to port and engage reverse gear?

MUST KNOW BEFORE YOU GO

THE ZIG ZAG SYNDROME: MOST COMMON PROBLEM FOR NEWCOMERS!

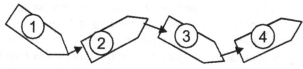

One of the most common problems for beginning boat dockers is steering in a straight line. We are used to an instant response to our commands when we drive our cars; boats, however, respond more casually. So neophytes inaccurately overcorrect, which makes matters worse, because now they must overcorrect in the opposite direction.

Experience indicates that patience and anticipation solves the problem. Allow the vessel time to respond before overloading with exaggerated input. Anticipating the next motion of your vessel also aids in alleviating the problem.

INTENDED DIRECTION

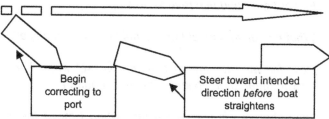

In the above graphic, the vessel is turning to starboard instead of going in the intended direction. Begin correcting direction by turning to port. As soon as boat moves into position slightly off center but still toward starboard, steer toward intended direction.

MUST KNOW BEFORE YOU GO

90% OF DOCKING IS ACCOMPLISHED IN NEUTRAL, WITH MOMENTUM MOVING/SLOWING VESSEL

Students are confused and puzzled when they hear that neutral is the dominant gear in the docking process. Observance of others indicates that docking is a whirlwind of violent voices, grinding gears, and lucky landings. But when done properly, docking is a smooth, stress-free exercise. Neutral gear allows the helmsman to assess external forces affecting the vessel's movement and it is the position from which corrections to direction are made.

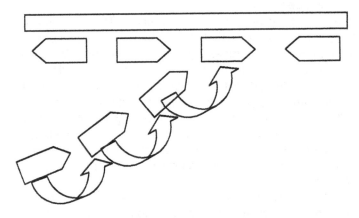

Engage Forward Gear
Immediately to Neutral
Momentum Moves Vessel to Next Position
Make Direction Correction
Engage Forward Gear, etc.

13

MUST KNOW BEFORE YOU GO

GO SLOW...NEUTRAL!!

Neutral, neutral, neutral!!.. When you are first learning to dock your boat, it is easy to get confused when the going gets tough. [This even occurs for us experienced dockers!] Neutral is home base; it is the place we go to when our responses are out of control or when we are unsure what to do next.

*Most control & tightest turns...*Going slow provides the most control, and we can make the tightest turns.

*Most ability to make minor corrections...*When we are going slow, the corrections we make will be minute in comparison to major corrections required when speeding.

*Easier to stop...*Stopping is quicker when we are moving at a slow speed.

*If you hit something, minimum damage...*There are some skippers who believe that if you have not hit something during the docking process, you haven't docked. While we fully respect some of their opinions and skills, we personally struggle with this type of ding/bang docking. If we hit something during the docking process, we think we failed. However, if you do hit something going slow, it is a heck of a lot better than hitting something when going fast.

*Better able to gauge wind or current...*Going slow allows you to assess how the wind/current will affect the docking process.

*When moving from forward to reverse or reverse to forward, no damage to transmission...*If you need to change gears from forward to reverse, or reverse to forward, you may do so when going slow, without risking damage to your transmission.

MUST KNOW BEFORE YOU GO

GO SLOW...NEUTRAL!!

React SOONER than you think you should...New dockers expect their boats to respond with the same instancy as their cars. Boats respond more casually; therefore, it is best to anticipate early and react sooner.

No hasty control actions...Some new dockers feel that they must ALWAYS be doing something at the helm. Sometimes it is best to do nothing. Making unnecessary direction corrections have gotten many new boaters into trouble.

If you start off wrong, START AGAIN...Many boaters feel embarrassed to back off an improperly-aligned docking attempt. So they stay with it, vrooming forward, shrieking into reverse, banging into this, dinging that, haplessly attempting to correct the uncorrectable. It is much easier, and more professional, to abort the ill-fated maneuver and begin over.

Never speed up and try to steer out of hitting something.. While it may seem appropriate at times to gun the throttle to avoid a collision, statistics prove otherwise. Too often, speeding up to avoid banging into something creates serious damage; much better to slow up and gently glide into contact with object [no arms or legs to slow contact].

ALWAYS protect your boat with fenders...Nearly all boaters will prepare their vessel for docking by placing fenders in collision-prone areas. However, too often, especially in transient slips, unanticipated occurrences expose "other" areas of vessels to dings. Therefore, it is prudent to protect boat on all sides. However, be sure that fender placement does not interfere with the docking process by getting caught on shoreside appendages.

MUST KNOW BEFORE YOU GO

SURGE OF POWER FROM NEUTRAL TO FORWARD OR REVERSE GEAR!

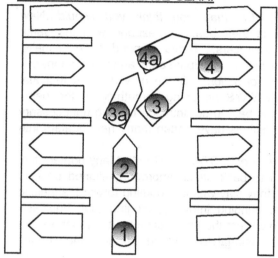

A surge in power occurs when we go from neutral to forward or reverse gear. This power surge is useful in boosting response for all boats, but vital for single-engine inboards. In the graphic above, a vessel is approaching a slip through a narrow lane, when a sharp turn is the difference between a successful or failed docking attempt. From position 2 to position 3a, the helmsman turned the wheel to starboard and went from neutral to forward, remaining in forward gear for turn. This resulted in a failed docking [position 4a], since the turn was not sharp enough for slip entry. However, if the helmsman had turned the wheel to starboard at position 2, and shifted back and forth rapidly between neutral and forward, using the power surge to boost the vessel thru the sharpened turn at position 3, he would have docked successfully at position 4.

MUST KNOW BEFORE YOU GO

MOST CONTROL WHEN BOW FACES INTO WIND!

It still amazes me when I experience the profound enhancement in control as I turn a vessel bow into the wind, even when the wind feels slight. It makes great sense. Wind wants to push and control your boat, and it is successful when it hits you on the sides or stern of your vessel. But you win the battle of the breezes when you face your bow into the howler. Now the wind wants to force you backwards, but the bow splits its force, and you battle back with your gear, negating its power. Therefore, you will have the most control when your bow faces into the wind.

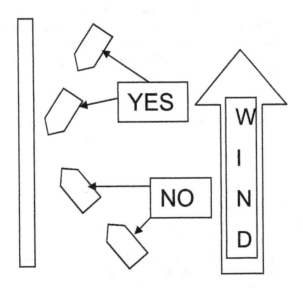

MUST KNOW BEFORE YOU GO

ADDITIONAL   MANEUVERING   POWER   IS   OBTAINED BY POSITIONING WHEEL FIRST, THEN ADDING POWER!

When changing vessel direction, ALWAYS turn the wheel FIRST, then add power. This is especially effective when you begin the direction change from neutral, since that burst of power discussed previously when moving from neutral to forward gear will enhance the responsiveness of your vessel.

YOUR SLIP ASSIGNMENT CAN MAKE DOCKING EASY OR DIFFICULT!

There are slip assignments that can leave even the most experienced skipper's hair standing on end. There is a marina in the Norfolk, VA area that has slips which confound us every time.   Dodge the ferries, watch out for the fierce currents, look out for that vessel whose bow sticks out 6 feet beyond the ending of the slip, then squeeze in between two vessels at a 90° angle with only a few feet of clearance on all sides!!   Tell the marina personnel that you require an easily accessible slip.

LOOK FOR A REFERENCE POINT!

When you will be docking in the same slip or approaching the same dock frequently, it can be very helpful to find a stationary object on shore to use as a reference point for when to begin or end a turn, or to provide clues which will aid in your successful docking.

MUST KNOW BEFORE YOU GO

WORK WITH YOUR BOAT WHEN IT DEVELOPS A MIND OF ITS OWN!

When training new boaters, it is interesting to see that they have not yet developed a working relationship with their vessel. The boat is either with you or against you, and sometimes you have to heed its lead. So if you need your vessel to change direction, and it is resisting such change, it may be responding to subtle nuances which you cannot detect. Use the boat's intuition to your advantage and incorporate its desires into your maneuver. The graphic below illustrates:

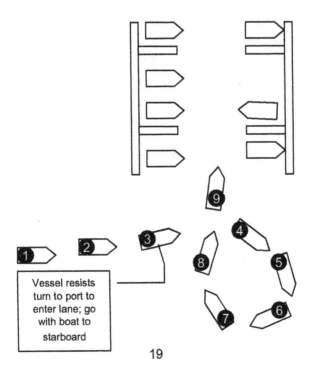

Vessel resists turn to port to enter lane; go with boat to starboard

19

MUST KNOW BEFORE YOU GO

SOMETIMES, IN ORDER TO CHANGE DIRECTION OF BACKWARD MOVEMENT, WE NEED TO USE FORWARD GEAR!

Forward gear is ALWAYS preferred over reverse gear, either because the vessel responds quicker or because we have a better view of our surroundings when looking forward. Therefore, it is preferable at times to correct backward direction by using forward gear. This is especially applicable with single-engine inboards, which can be unpredictable in reverse gear.

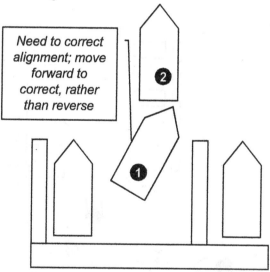

Need to correct alignment; move forward to correct, rather than reverse

MUST KNOW BEFORE YOU GO

DOCKING PLANS ARE AN ESSENTIAL PART OF DOCKING SUCCESSFULLY!

A docking plan consists of three important elements which will lead to consistent docking success.

Visualization: envisioning the layout of the marina or pier you are approaching is key to the docking plan. The entry and exit can be tricky, and finding the lane to your assigned slip in an unfamiliar facility can be unnerving. Get as much info on the arrangement as is available, and ask for details from marina staff before advancing.

Anticipation: foreseeing problem areas BEFORE they are encountered is crucial to docking, as well as boat handling in general. As you go over the facility layout, look for sections in which strong winds/currents are liable to push you off course, shallow areas, and/or segments in which close encounters with other vessels is likely.

Compensation: knowing how to offset each of the anticipated potential problems is the final part of the docking plan. What will you do if those strong winds/currents begin to blow you off course? How will you direct your vessel to avoid those shallow spots? When you encounter other vessels in that narrow lane, what will you do?

THE DOCKING PLAN EMPOWERS YOU!

THE DOCKING PLAN- CALM CONDITIONS

Visualization   Anticipation   Compensation

As demonstrated in the graphic below, the Docking Plan would prepare the helmsman for possible encounters at the fuel dock, close-quarter situations at the turn, and shallow water as indicated.

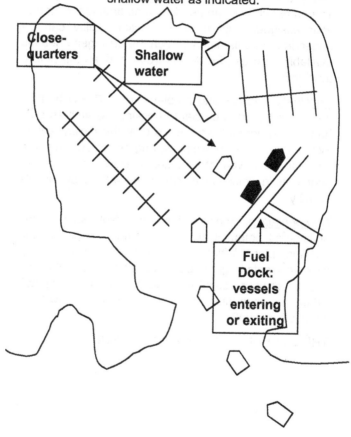

Close-quarters

Shallow water

Fuel Dock: vessels entering or exiting

DOCKING

GENERICS

DOCKING GENERICS

DOCKING TECHNIQUES – CALM CONDITIONS!

REMINDER: See line handling section for detailed explanation of lines.

APPROACHING EMPTY FUEL DOCK OR PIER

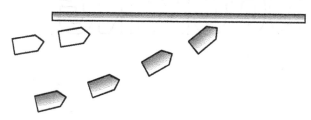

The lighter vessel is approaching the empty fuel dock too close to the dock. A wake from another vessel. a burst of wind, or a hardly discernable current, could push it into the dock prematurely. The darker vessel has the proper alignment for the safest approach.

APPROACHING CROWDED FUEL DOCK OR PIER

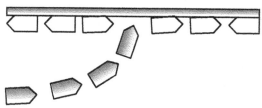

Note that the darker vessel approaches a good distance away from the docked vessels to avoid close encounters. The darker vessel points its bow at the indicated angle to the dock so that the line handler can pass the spring line, and an additional stern line*, to the dockhand, thus preventing the vessel from running into the docked vessels on either side. [*See graphic on next page.]

DOCKING GENERICS

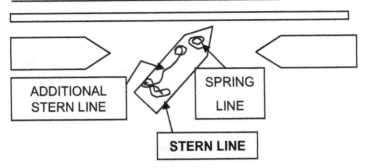

ADDITIONAL STERN LINE

SPRING LINE

STERN LINE

[Details on lines & line handling may be found under Line Handlers/Dockhands.]

One of the problems with handing off the spring line only to the dockhand is that the line handler must then rush to the back of the vessel and throw the stern line to the dockhand. Too often it winds up in the drink, and the stern can be difficult to bring to the dock in such close quarters by the helmsman alone. Therefore, in a close quarters situation, the line handler should prepare the additional stern line before approach, and hand the dockhand both the spring and stern lines from the bow.

If there is no dockhand on shore, the line handler can step off with both the spring line and stern line in hand. The spring line should be tied off first, so that the helmsman can use the spring line to help bring the stern to the dock or pier [especially with single-engine inboards]. This is done by turning the wheel away from the dock or pier, applying forward gear and immediately to neutral, pushing against spring line to bring stern in. The line handler, who has the additional stern line in hand, helps the helmsman into position.

DOCKING GENERICS

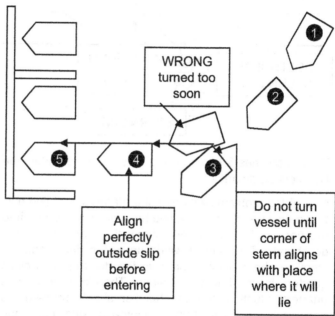

WRONG
turned too
soon

Align
perfectly
outside slip
before
entering

Do not turn
vessel until
corner of
stern aligns
with place
where it will
lie

When docking bow-in in calm conditions, it is important to align the vessel perfectly outside the slip BEFORE beginning entry into slip. Also, it is beneficial to find a reference point on shore which marks the place at which to begin the turn into the slip.

The most common error the helmsman makes is that he turns prematurely at position 3, creating wrong alignment. Holding until the corner of the stern aligns with the place at which it will lie when in the slip insures successful docking. It is a sharp, quick turn from position 3 to position 4.

DOCKING GENERICS

DOCKING STERN IN – CALM CONDITIONS!

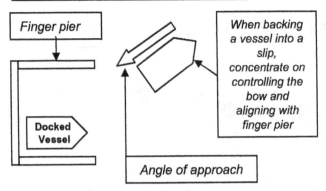

Finger pier

Docked Vessel

When backing a vessel into a slip, concentrate on controlling the bow and aligning with finger pier

Angle of approach

Backing a vessel into a slip stern-in is the most difficult maneuver in boating. For many vessels, reverse is the least controllable gear, and this is compounded by the fact that we have less favorable visibility when backing our vessel. In addition, many vessels today are built as lightly as possible so that they can go faster more efficiently, which means that the bow of the boat gets pushed around even in light wind/current. And the icing on the cake is that manufacturers, in their effort to provide as much interior space as possible, removed the outside walkways, thereby inhibiting the line handlers' ability to move quickly between bow and stern, as needed during the docking process.

Because of the aforementioned info, it is important to focus on the essential elements and forget the others. In the graphic above, many helmsmen become preoccupied with avoiding the docked vessel. This distracts them from the task at hand: being sure the bow doesn't blow out of control and aligning with the finger pier. So gauge the angle at which to approach the finger pier and let the line handler provide feedback on your proximity to the docked vessel. If your alignment is correct, you will not hit the docked vessel.

DOCKING GENERICS

DOCKING STERN-IN – CALM CONDITIONS!

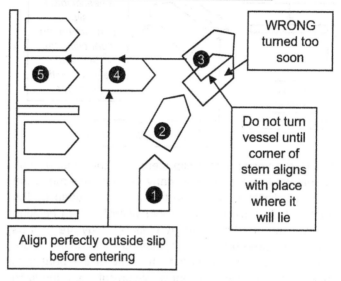

When docking stern-in in calm conditions, it is important to align the vessel perfectly outside the slip BEFORE beginning entry into slip. Also, it is beneficial to find a reference point on shore which marks the place at which to begin the turn into the slip.

The most common error the helmsman makes is that he turns prematurely at position 3, creating wrong alignment. Holding until the corner of the stern aligns with the place at which it will lie when in the slip insures successful docking. It is a sharp, quick turn from position 3 to position 4.

28

UNDOCKING

GENERICS

UNDOCKING GENERICS

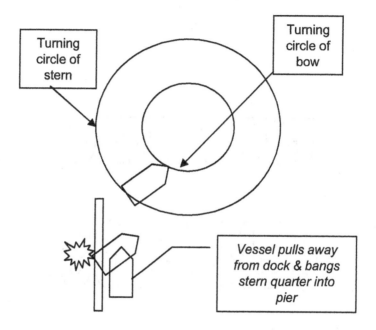

Turning circle of stern

Turning circle of bow

Vessel pulls away from dock & bangs stern quarter into pier

Boat purchasers are told that boats steer like cars. While there are a few similarities, there are way many more differences. In particular, roads don't move and water does, plus wind rarely blows autos off the road, but boats are frequently pushed off course by the breezes.

When we drive our cars, we rarely look behind to see whether or not the back of the car is following. However, in order for the bow of the boat to turn to starboard, the stern of the boat, which controls direction, must turn to port. And the stern needs a wider turning circle. Many skippers do not recognize this fact, as demonstrated by the fact that more than 25% of vessels show damage to stern quarter.

UNDOCKING GENERICS

Undocking a vessel should ALWAYS be done as follows, regardless of type of vessel.

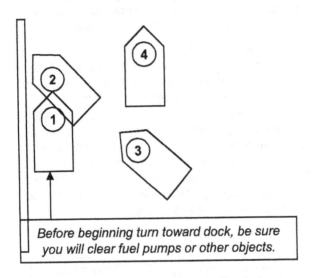

Before beginning turn toward dock, be sure you will clear fuel pumps or other objects.

Position 1 – vessel at fuel dock or pier, ready to undock. Helmsman directs bow toward dock and into Position 2, carefully avoiding fuel pumps or any other objects.

Position 2 - vessel with bow pointing toward dock begins backing into Position 3. Be sure to back a sufficient distance from pier or other vessels, to avoid any close quarters encounters.

Position 3 – after assuring that there are no other boats or objects interfering with the maneuver, vessel moves into Position 4, and pulls away.

WIND & CURRENT

Wind & current are the bane of boat docking. Even experienced helmsmen get sweaty palms in direct proportion to the breezes, and strong currents have left them white-knuckled on many occasions.

The first step to handling wind/current is to discern it. Position a flag on your vessel that will aid in your assessment of the wind direction, being sure to take your own vessel's movement into consideration. Some skippers have installed an anemometer, which will gauge wind speed as well as direction. Assess the current by noticing its telltale sign around pilings or buoys. The best way to measure their effect on your vessel is to slow up in an open area nearby your docking site and note how your vessel is moving in response to these forces.

Current Flow

CURRENT: buoy leans away from current direction; ripples pronounced on opposite side of current direction.

Even slight wind/current can alter the technique required for successful docking. The lighter your vessel, the higher the hull structure above the water, the more plastic enclosures on the upper helm station, the more your vessel will be pushed by the wind, instead of heeding your directions. Conversely, the deeper your draft, the greater your keel, the more the current will affect your boat.

WIND & CURRENT

Wind/current will cause your boat to respond differently than in calm conditions. Depending upon the weight of your vessel and its configuration, even very light winds/current can have a profound effect. It will be necessary to modify approach, maneuvering, and line-handling.

Determine what effect wind/current will have on your docking site during the planning stage. A simple act in calm conditions, such as entering the aisle/fairway to your slip, becomes precarious as the wind/current pushes you closer than you want to be to the docked vessels along the way.

There is a tremendous advantage to stopping close to final position and judging effect of wind/current for accurate adjustments. Knowing in advance how the boat will be affected allows us to determine how far and when to turn the wheel, or how much throttle to apply and when to apply it. We could ascertain the appropriate angle of approach so as to avoid nearby vessels and determine how to use the wind/current to our advantage. However, it has been my experience that in many situations, if I have arrived at my slip entrance in nasty conditions, the risk of slowing up to determine affect may be greater than following my predetermined docking plan.

Do all that you can to keep the bow into the wind during the bulk of your maneuvering. Second best position is stern into the wind, especially when backing. Avoid putting the port/starboard side into the wind. One of my most challenging docking experiences occurred in

WIND & CURRENT

brisk winds in northern Florida, where currents were also at play. The graphic below illustrates my dilemma.

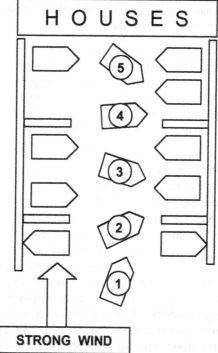

The wind caught our stern on the starboard side and moved us into position 2. We attempted to correct but were blown into position 3. The wind was so strong on the starboard side that our correction attempts were nullified into position 4. We had to use full throttle to get the vessel into position 5, thus avoiding the houses on shore.

WIND & CURRENT

Had to use full throttle to gain control of the boat in strong winds and current. This is the most formidable challenge to docking in wind/current. Forget the awesome control and finesse of docking in calm conditions. No matter how great your boat handling skills in calm conditions, docking in wind/current is a different game, and it can be unforgiving. That is why it is so imperative to learn slowly, and build your skills and confidence gradually. In wind/current you have to think quickly, act immediately, and know your vessel's responses without doubt. You must have the prior docking experiences because in wind/current, you are more or less acting on instinct, and "feeling" the appropriate positioning of the boat.

The bow of your boat will get pushed downwind before the stern. When backing with wind/current, it is easy to become preoccupied with aligning the stern properly and forget the bow. Controlling the bow in strong winds, especially in light vessels, is the key to successfully docking your vessel stern in. You can align your vessel perfectly to back into the slip but if the wind catches the bow, it will sabotage your docking attempt.

Docking in wind/current is discussed in detail in the section of this book which relates to individual boat types. Whenever wind alone is referred to in the text, it should be interpreted as wind or current.

WIND & CURRENT

THE DOCKING PLAN – WITH WIND/CURRENT

Visualization   Anticipation   Compensation

As demonstrated in the graphic below, the Docking Plan would prepare the helmsman for wind-blown encounters with docked vessels, fuel dock exiters, and alter docking approach.

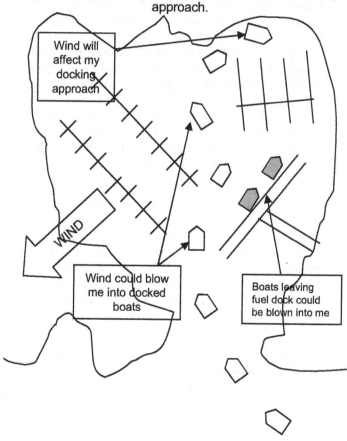

Wind will affect my docking approach

WIND

Wind could blow me into docked boats

Boats leaving fuel dock could be blown into me

LINE HANDLERS & DOCKHANDS

Line handlers & dockhands can make or break your docking plan. Directions to the line handler comes from the helmsperson at the planning stage, not yelled at the docking stage. The line handler is not the person who should be blamed if things go awry; however, he/she should understand the role and responsibilities. Conversely, the line handler is not the person in control of the vessel and should not dictate orders to the helm.

The most important part of the line handler's job on large vessels is to provide feedback to the helmsperson, especially when backing the boat, since visibility may be impaired or non-existent. *How far am I from the finger pier? How close am I to the vessel docked beside me? How much further must I back to be in final position?*

The line handler should have a fender in hand during the docking process. The fender can be placed in a position to protect the vessel in case of close encounters. Arms or legs should never be used to prevent a ding.

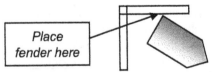

Place fender here

Having the lines in the proper position, of the correct length and breadth, is also an essential part of the line handler's responsibility. Especially in wind/current, the line handler must act quickly. The helmsman must place the boat in a position where the line handler can step off, but this must be done expeditiously when the breezes are blowing. Once again, practicing in calm conditions will prepare all parties for the more challenging aspects of docking. While undocking, the line handler must watch that no line falls into the water and fouls the propeller.

LINE HANDLERS & DOCKHANDS

Line handlers should know the proper way to coil a line so that they can toss it to shore without it falling into the water and winding around the prop.

COILING A LINE!
If the line is free, you may begin coiling at either end. If one end is cleated, start at the end that is secured.

Start coiling here and work toward here

Twisted line will coil in loops, while braided line will coil into figure 8s.[Details on docking lines may be found on page 42.]

With twisted line, run the line through your hands from the start to the finish, squeezing out any kinks or tangles. Hold the twisted or braided line in your least preferred hand and make a **clockwise** loop about 3 feet long with your preferred hand. Bring the loop or coil to the least preferred hand and hold it in that hand. Make another loop in the same way, and lay it *next to* the first loop, being sure not to overlap the first one. Continue the clockwise loops until the line is completely coiled. Carefully hand off the coiled rows to the throwing hand and toss it to shore.

LINE HANDLERS & DOCKHANDS

The coiled line should be <u>under</u> the rail on the boat. [See graphic below.] If the line goes over the rail, the rail could bend or snap if the line is under pressure.

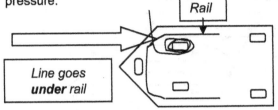

Line goes **under** rail

Line handlers and dockhands should not tie off lines too tightly, or the helmsman could lose the ability to maneuver. The graphic below describes a common erroneous scenario:

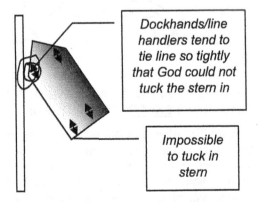

Dockhands/line handlers tend to tie line so tightly that God could not tuck the stern in

Impossible to tuck in stern

Some helmsmen are so concerned about lines being secured improperly that they ask the line handlers not to pass the lines to the dockhand until they are sure they are positioned correctly.

LINE HANDLERS & DOCKHANDS

TYING DOCKING LINES!

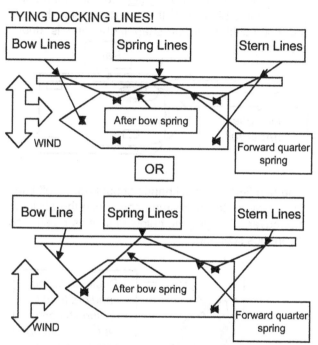

FIRST LINE ASHORE WITH WIND FROM ALL DIRECTIONS <u>EXCEPT</u> FROM STERN:

Bow-In: The after bow spring line is the first line to be handed or fastened ashore when the wind is from any direction, except from the stern. The after bow spring line allows the helmsman to make adjustments at the bow and stern with ease.

Stern-In: Use the forward quarter spring in place of after bow spring.

LINE HANDLERS & DOCKHANDS

TYING DOCKING LINES!

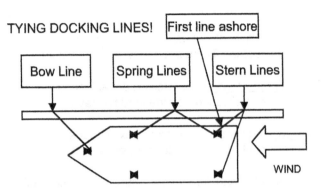

FIRST LINE ASHORE WITH WIND FROM STERN:

The stern line is the first line to be handed or fastened ashore when the wind is from the stern. The stern line allows the helmsman to hold the vessel to the finger pier or dock while making adjustments at the bow and stern with ease.

DOCKING LINES

Nylon line is best: it is strong, stretches, and is sunlight resistant. There are two types of nylon line:

Three-Strand Twisted: stretchier, doesn't snag, costs less; recommended for travel

Braided: slightly stronger, more flexible, looks cool, recommended for permanent slip

Line diameter and length are critical to successful and safe docking. Use the following table as a guide:

LINE DIAMETER	BOAT LENGTH
3/8"	up to 25'
1/2"	up to 35'
5/8"	up to 45'
3/4"	up to 55'
7/8"	up to 65'

EYE SPLICE vs KNOTS

An eye splice is MUCH stronger than a knot. A 12" eye is a perfect size. When at your home dock, it is advisable to leave the eye splice on the boat so that you may make adjustments to the line after you step ashore or when you arrive at your vessel. On the other hand, it is suggested that the eye splice goes ashore when at a transient slip so that you can adjust free end from your vessel.

DOCKING LINES

The length and condition of docking lines determines whether or not your boat stays in place safely. The following are suggested lengths for the various lines used on your vessel:

Bow & stern lines: 2/3 of boat's length
Spring lines: same length as boat
Piling lines: same length as boat
Short lines: prime cause of damage

Use chafe protection where abrasion occurs. A cleat or chock rubbing against the line in the same place can damage the fibers and weaken the line. Plastic or rubber hoses can be slipped over the line, waterproof tape, or any of the numerous commercial chafe protection products can protect the line, and your boat, from harm.

THE 7 STEPS

1 Read & review Skill Drills on land

2 Practice Skill Drills on water

3 Formulate a Docking Plan

4 Bring vessel to dock or pier - no wind or current

5 Bring vessel bow into slip – no wind or current

6 Bring vessel stern into slip – no wind or current

7 Dock vessel with wind &/or current

VARIOUS BOAT TYPES HANDLE DIFFERENTLY
DURING THE DOCKING PROCESS!

Therefore, following are details on the nuances of
handling each of the various boat types. They are
divided into three sections:

Vessels with Inboard Single Engines

Vessels with Outboard,, Inboard/Outboard [I/O],
Stern-Drive, Single Engines

Vessels with Inboard/Outboard Twin Engines

INBOARD

SINGLE

ENGINE

INBOARD, SINGLE ENGINE

Single-engine inboards have five components which play a role in the boat docking process.

Neutral Gear – Momentum Moving Vessel

Steering Wheel or Tiller*

Forward Gear

Reverse Gear

Throttle

A sixth component is available, if the throttle and gear shift are in separate handles.

Pre-Set RPMs

*Comments regarding steering will be made from the perspective of a steering wheel. The tiller is turned in the opposite direction from the vessel movement.

INBOARD, SINGLE ENGINE

Neutral Gear – Momentum Moving Vessel

90% of the boat docking process is done in neutral, with momentum moving vessel to its destination. Neutral gear separates the pros from the neophytes. The only time the vessel is in any other gear is to keep the vessel moving, change the direction, or overcome wind/current.

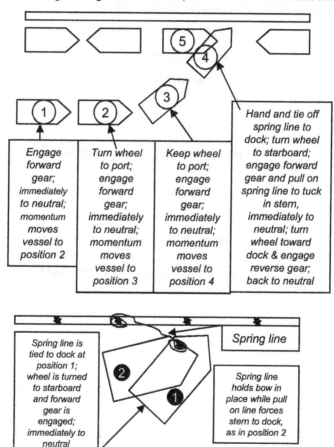

Engage forward gear; immediately to neutral; momentum moves vessel to position 2	Turn wheel to port; engage forward gear; immediately to neutral; momentum moves vessel to position 3	Keep wheel to port; engage forward gear; immediately to neutral; momentum moves vessel to position 4	Hand and tie off spring line to dock; turn wheel to starboard; engage forward gear and pull on spring line to tuck in stern, immediately to neutral; turn wheel toward dock & engage reverse gear; back to neutral

Spring line is tied to dock at position 1; wheel is turned to starboard and forward gear is engaged; immediately to neutral

Spring line

Spring line holds bow in place while pull on line forces stern to dock, as in position 2

INBOARD, SINGLE ENGINE

Steering Wheel or Tiller
The steering wheel or tiller play a vital role in the docking process. To be most effective in changing direction, the wheel or tiller should be turned in the appropriate direction BEFORE engaging gear.

Forward Gear
Forward gear is very critical in single-engine inboards, beyond their usual role. Obviously, they move the vessel in a forward direction. However, since reverse gear is so unpredictable and sluggish to respond, forward gear is also used to correct backward direction.

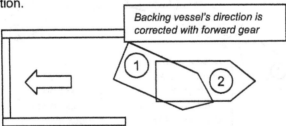

Backing vessel's direction is corrected with forward gear

Many single-engine inboard vessels choose to dock bow-in to a slip. Since a surge of power is released in the first few seconds when going from neutral to forward gear, that burst of power is repeated rapidly to turn the boat sharply into the slip.

INBOARD, SINGLE ENGINE

Reverse gear

Single engine inboards will back to either starboard or port, depending upon the direction the propeller turns. Right hand props move bow to port in forward, stern to port in reverse [LHP opposite]. Backing up is most difficult to control. In open water, with wheel centered, see which direction the vessel turns when reversed. Use that backing direction to your advantage.

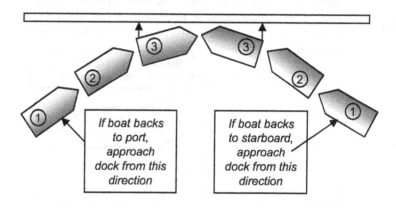

If boat backs to port, approach dock from this direction

If boat backs to starboard, approach dock from this direction

Throttle

The throttle is only used to overcome wind or current. Apply the throttle sparingly, since it tends to grow in intensity if overused. First we move quickly to port, then we must overact to starboard, etc.

50

INBOARD, SINGLE ENGINE

Preset RPMs

Preset rpms may only be useful if your vessel has a separate shift for gear and throttle. If the gear and throttle are in the same handle, this component of docking is unavailable to you.

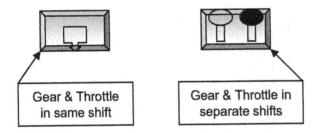

| Gear & Throttle in same shift | Gear & Throttle in separate shifts |

The purpose of presetting rpms is to provide additional maneuvering power when docking your vessel. Before raising rpms, check your engine manual for the highest throttle rpms in which gears can be safely changed from forward to reverse without damaging the transmission.

What we are actually doing here is the equivalent of pressing your foot on the gas pedal of your car while in neutral, and before putting it in drive. This is extremely effective in handling single-engine inboards, since the gear shift alone may then manage to overcome wind and/or current, without having to use the throttle.

Set-up the preset rpms when the vessel is in neutral. Move the throttle shift forward until the manufacturer's maximum level is reached. Then, use your gear shift as needed to successfully dock your boat.

INBOARD, SINGLE ENGINE

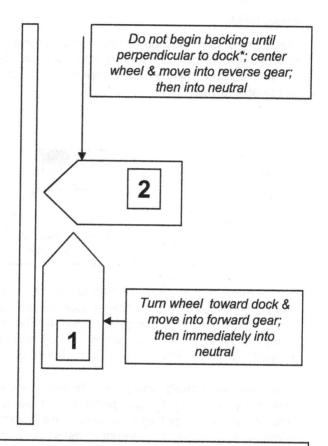

Do not begin backing until perpendicular to dock*; center wheel & move into reverse gear; then into neutral

2

Turn wheel toward dock & move into forward gear; then immediately into neutral

1

*Since vessel may back unpredictably, it is important to back from this exaggerated position to avoid hitting other vessels at dock.

REMINDER: watch for fuel pumps and/or pumpouts on dock

INBOARD, SINGLE ENGINE

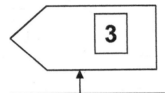

Allow momentum to bring you to
position 3; then turn wheel to
starboard, move into forward gear,
and pull away

UNDOCKING

INBOARD, SINGLE ENGINE

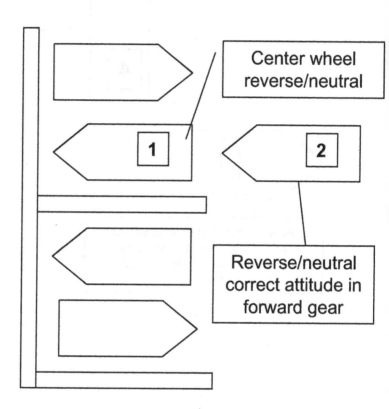

Center wheel
reverse/neutral

1

2

Reverse/neutral
correct attitude in
forward gear

LEAVING

INBOARD, SINGLE ENGINE

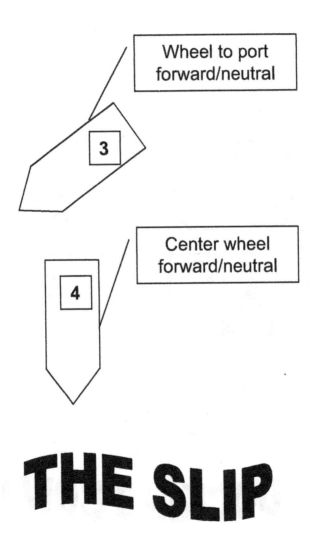

Wheel to port
forward/neutral

3

Center wheel
forward/neutral

4

THE SLIP

INBOARD, SINGLE ENGINE

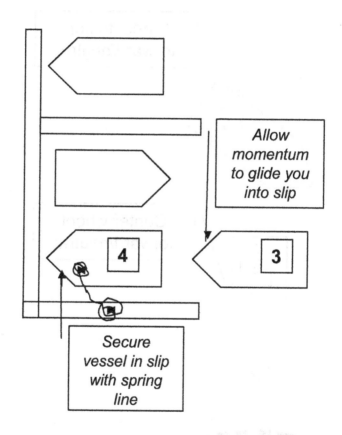

Allow momentum to glide you into slip

4

3

Secure vessel in slip with spring line

DOCKING BOW-IN

INBOARD, SINGLE ENGINE

Place fenders on both sides of vessel; turn wheel to starboard when stern of vessel aligns with final position in slip*; engage forward gear; back to neutral

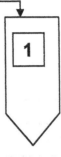

Stern of vessel is in alignment

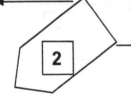

In neutral, engage forward gear; back to neutral; repeat rapidly between neutral and forward until vessel turns into proper alignment; center wheel

*Look for reference point on shore

CALM CONDITIONS

57

INBOARD, SINGLE ENGINE

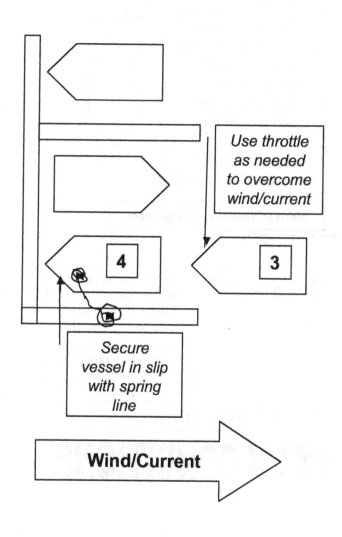

Use throttle
as needed
to overcome
wind/current

4

3

Secure
vessel in slip
with spring
line

Wind/Current

INBOARD, SINGLE ENGINE

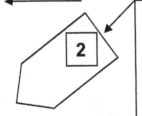

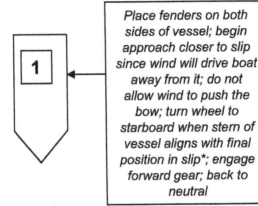

Place fenders on both sides of vessel; begin approach closer to slip since wind will drive boat away from it; do not allow wind to push the bow; turn wheel to starboard when stern of vessel aligns with final position in slip*; engage forward gear; back to neutral

Stern of vessel is in alignment

In neutral, engage forward gear; back to neutral; repeat rapidly between neutral and forward until vessel turns into proper alignment; use throttle as needed to overcome wind/current; center wheel

*Look for reference point on shore

BOW-IN

INBOARD, SINGLE ENGINE

Approach at angle indicated and use wind to glide vessel into slip; get at least half vessel into slip before wind overpowers; use throttle sparingly; adjust wheel as needed; line handler quickly steps off at bow

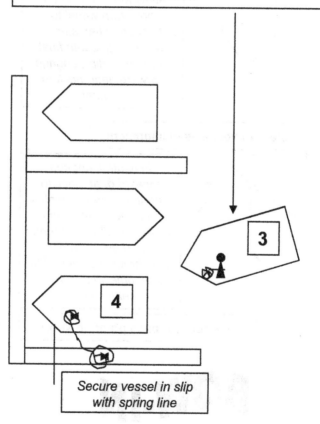

3

4

Secure vessel in slip with spring line

INBOARD, SINGLE ENGINE

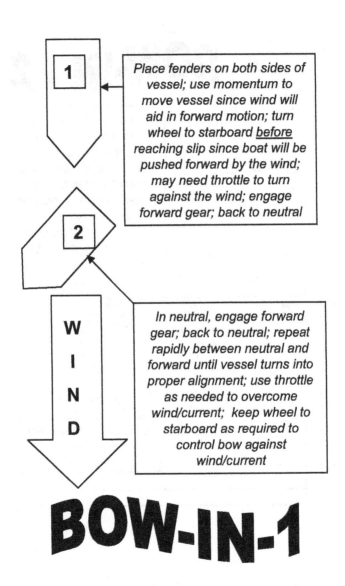

1 Place fenders on both sides of vessel; use momentum to move vessel since wind will aid in forward motion; turn wheel to starboard <u>before</u> reaching slip since boat will be pushed forward by the wind; may need throttle to turn against the wind; engage forward gear; back to neutral

2 In neutral, engage forward gear; back to neutral; repeat rapidly between neutral and forward until vessel turns into proper alignment; use throttle as needed to overcome wind/current; keep wheel to starboard as required to control bow against wind/current

W I N D

BOW-IN-1

BOW-IN - 2

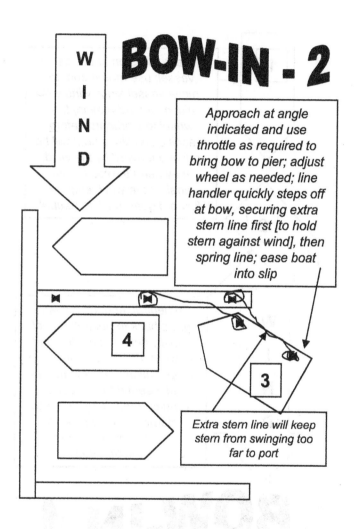

WIND

Approach at angle indicated and use throttle as required to bring bow to pier; adjust wheel as needed; line handler quickly steps off at bow, securing extra stern line first [to hold stern against wind], then spring line; ease boat into slip

4

3

Extra stern line will keep stern from swinging too far to port

INBOARD, SINGLE ENGINE

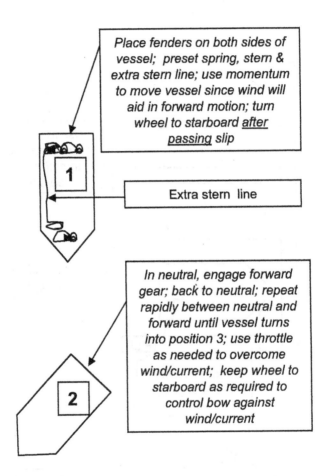

Place fenders on both sides of vessel; preset spring, stern & extra stern line; use momentum to move vessel since wind will aid in forward motion; turn wheel to starboard _after_ _passing_ slip

1

Extra stern line

In neutral, engage forward gear; back to neutral; repeat rapidly between neutral and forward until vessel turns into position 3; use throttle as needed to overcome wind/current; keep wheel to starboard as required to control bow against wind/current

2

INBOARD, SINGLE ENGINE

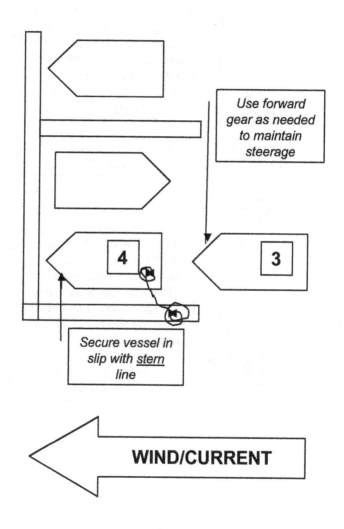

Use forward gear as needed to maintain steerage

Secure vessel in slip with _stern_ line

WIND/CURRENT

INBOARD, SINGLE ENGINE

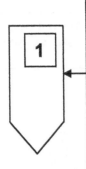

1

Place fenders on both sides of vessel; begin approach further from slip since wind will drive boat towards it; do not allow wind to push the bow; turn wheel to starboard when stern of vessel aligns with final position in slip*; engage forward gear; back to neutral

Stern of vessel is in alignment

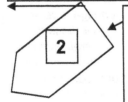

2

In neutral, engage forward gear; back to neutral; repeat rapidly between neutral and forward until vessel turns into proper alignment; use throttle sparingly, since wind will aid in driving boat to slip; center wheel

*Look for reference point on shore

BOW-IN

INBOARD, SINGLE ENGINE

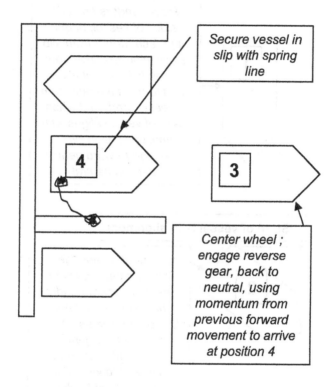

Secure vessel in slip with spring line

4

3

Center wheel ; engage reverse gear, back to neutral, using momentum from previous forward movement to arrive at position 4

DOCKING STERN-IN

INBOARD, SINGLE ENGINE

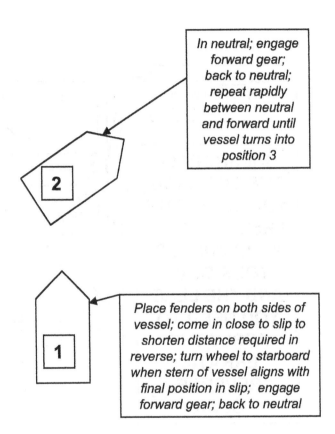

In neutral; engage forward gear; back to neutral; repeat rapidly between neutral and forward until vessel turns into position 3

2

Place fenders on both sides of vessel; come in close to slip to shorten distance required in reverse; turn wheel to starboard when stern of vessel aligns with final position in slip; engage forward gear; back to neutral

1

CALM CONDITIONS

INBOARD, SINGLE ENGINE

Get _stern_ line on
quickly to hold vessel
in slip

THE SHORTER
THE DISTANCE
YOU BACK, THE
LESS TIME THE
WIND PUSHES
YOUR BOW,
AND THE LESS
YOU NEED TO
APPLY THE
ERRATIC
REVERSE
GEAR

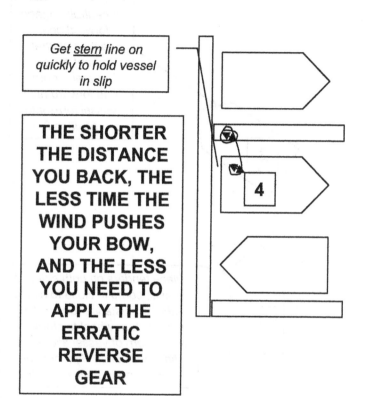

4

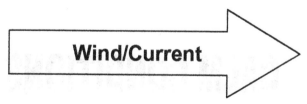

Wind/Current

INBOARD, SINGLE ENGINE

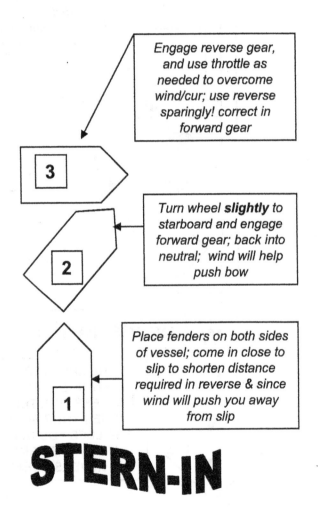

3 → Engage reverse gear, and use throttle as needed to overcome wind/cur; use reverse sparingly! correct in forward gear

2 → Turn wheel **slightly** to starboard and engage forward gear; back into neutral; wind will help push bow

1 → Place fenders on both sides of vessel; come in close to slip to shorten distance required in reverse & since wind will push you away from slip

STERN-IN

INBOARD, SINGLE ENGINE

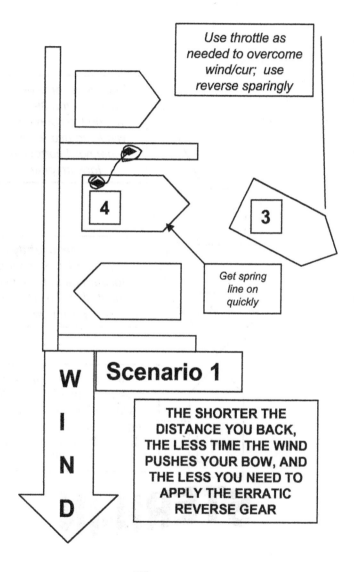

Use throttle as needed to overcome wind/cur; use reverse sparingly

4

3

Get spring line on quickly

W
I
N
D

Scenario 1

THE SHORTER THE DISTANCE YOU BACK, THE LESS TIME THE WIND PUSHES YOUR BOW, AND THE LESS YOU NEED TO APPLY THE ERRATIC REVERSE GEAR

INBOARD, SINGLE ENGINE

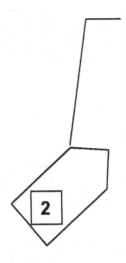

Let bow pass slip before beginning turn; turn wheel slightly to starboard; wind will whip bow quickly to starboard so immediately turn wheel to port and engage reverse gear; before shifting into reverse, you will need sufficient speed during the forward turn to overcome the wind/current in reverse

Place fenders on both sides of vessel; come in close to slip to shorten distance required in reverse; forward, neutral; do not allow wind to catch the bow

STERN-IN

INBOARD, SINGLE ENGINE

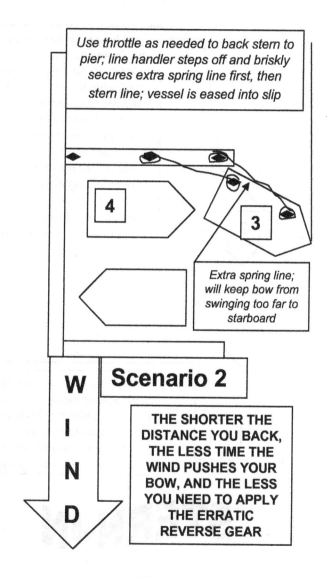

Use throttle as needed to back stern to pier; line handler steps off and briskly secures extra spring line first, then stern line; vessel is eased into slip

4

3

Extra spring line; will keep bow from swinging too far to starboard

W
I
N
D

Scenario 2

THE SHORTER THE DISTANCE YOU BACK, THE LESS TIME THE WIND PUSHES YOUR BOW, AND THE LESS YOU NEED TO APPLY THE ERRATIC REVERSE GEAR

INBOARD, SINGLE ENGINE

Let bow pass slip before beginning turn; turn wheel slightly to starboard; wind will whip bow quickly to starboard so immediately turn wheel to port and engage reverse gear; before shifting into reverse, build up sufficient speed in forward turn to overcome wind/current in reverse

2

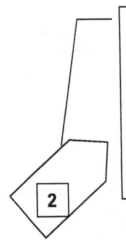

Place fenders on both sides of vessel; come in close to slip to shorten distance required in reverse; spring & stern lines are preset; bring a second spring line from bow to stern; forward, neutral; do not allow wind to catch the bow

1

Extra spring line

STERN-IN

INBOARD, SINGLE ENGINE

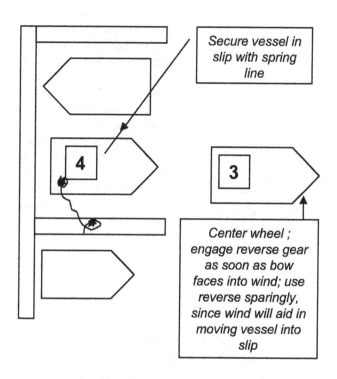

Secure vessel in slip with spring line

4

3

Center wheel ; engage reverse gear as soon as bow faces into wind; use reverse sparingly, since wind will aid in moving vessel into slip

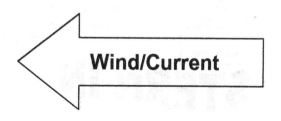

Wind/Current

74

INBOARD, SINGLE ENGINE

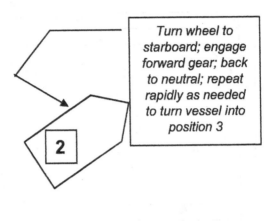

Turn wheel to starboard; engage forward gear; back to neutral; repeat rapidly as needed to turn vessel into position 3

2

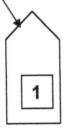

Place fenders on both sides of vessel; come in further from slip since wind will push you toward slip; use enough speed to maintain direction

1

STERN-IN

INBOARD, SINGLE ENGINE

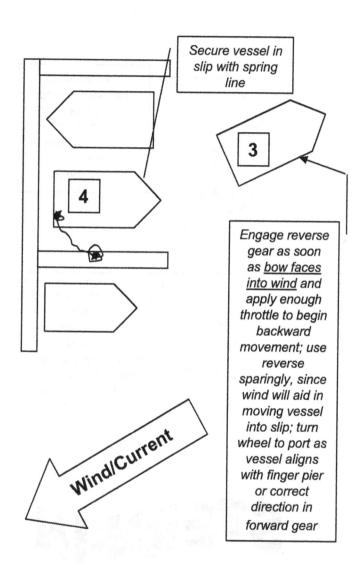

Secure vessel in slip with spring line

3

4

Engage reverse gear as soon as _bow faces into wind_ and apply enough throttle to begin backward movement; use reverse sparingly, since wind will aid in moving vessel into slip; turn wheel to port as vessel aligns with finger pier or correct direction in forward gear

Wind/Current

INBOARD, SINGLE ENGINE

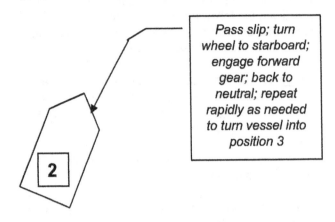

Pass slip; turn wheel to starboard; engage forward gear; back to neutral; repeat rapidly as needed to turn vessel into position 3

2

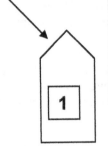

Place fenders on both sides of vessel; come in further from slip since wind will push you toward slip; use enough speed to maintain direction

1

STERN-IN

INBOARD, SINGLE ENGINE

SKILL DRILLS

Build the muscles of successful boat docking by practicing the following on the water:

Get close enough to any object so you can judge boat movement, but not close enough to hit.

Stage 1*: concentration on development of boat control skills in calm conditions, no wind/current. Use gear shifts & steering wheel only; no throttle. Note boat's reaction after each gear change.*

Start and stop in forward gear, with steering wheel centered [using reverse to stop]

Start and stop in reverse gear, with steering wheel centered [using forward to stop]

Align bow with stationary object; steering wheel centered; start in forward gear and return to neutral; let momentum continue to move boat forward until steerage is lost or vessel stops; hold vessel in same position

Align stern with stationary object; steering wheel centered; start in reverse gear and return to neutral; let momentum continue to move boat backwards until steerage is lost or vessel stops; hold vessel in same position

[Idle speed means no throttle, just going to forward or reverse gear. The following turns to port or starboard are begun by turning wheel in appropriate direction BEFORE engaging gear.]

Turn to port in forward gear at continuous idle speed [note arc]

INBOARD, SINGLE ENGINE

SKILL DRILLS

Turn to port in forward gear at intermittent idle speed [forward/neutral, forward/neutral] [note arc]

Turn to starboard in forward gear at continuous idle speed [note arc]

Turn to starboard in forward gear at intermittent idle speed [forward/neutral, forward/neutral] [note arc]

Turn to port in reverse gear at continuous idle speed [note arc]

Turn to port in reverse gear at intermittent idle speed [reverse/neutral, reverse/neutral] [note arc]

Turn to starboard in reverse gear at continuous idle speed [note arc]

Turn to starboard in reverse gear at intermittent idle speed [reverse/neutral, reverse/neutral] [note arc]

Turn to port in forward gear at intermittent idle speed, then shift into reverse and note boat reaction

Turn to starboard in forward gear at intermittent idle speed, then shift into reverse and note boat reaction

Practice boat's turning circle to port in forward gear

Practice boat's turning circle to port in forward gear, sharpening turn by moving back and forth between forward and reverse

INBOARD, SINGLE ENGINE

SKILL DRILLS

Practice   boat's turning circle to starboard in forward gear

Practice boat's turning circle to starboard in forward gear, sharpening turn by moving back and forth between forward and reverse

Practice boat's turning circle to port in reverse gear

Practice boat's turning circle to port in reverse gear, sharpening turn by moving back and forth between forward and reverse

Practice   boat's turning circle to starboard in reverse gear

Practice boat's turning circle to starboard in reverse gear, sharpening turn by moving back and forth between forward and reverse

Practice bringing boat to full stop with varying amounts of speed, including full speed

Practice all maneuvers again, but put vessel into neutral after each gear engagement and let boat's momentum move vessel until she begins to stop or lose steerage

INBOARD, SINGLE ENGINE

SKILL DRILLS

Stage 2: *concentration on development of boat control skills with wind/current. Stage 2 skill development uses gear shift, steering wheel and throttle for steering.*

If gear shift and throttle are in one handle, throttle is applied by additional movement forward or reverse. Use only enough throttle to overcome effects of wind/current.

Practice the Stage 1 skill drills, applying throttle after each gear shift change.

If gear shift and throttle are in separate handles, see section on inboard single-engines, preset rpms.

Practice the Stage 1 skill drills, with raised rpms, then repractice, adding throttle after each gear shift change.

OUTBOARD, I/O, STERN-DRIVE

Vessels with Outboard, Inboard/Outboard [I/O], Stern-Drive, Single Engines all handle similarly. They have five components which play a role in the boat docking process.

Forward Gear

Reverse Gear

Neutral Gear – Momentum Slowing Vessel

Steering Wheel

Throttle

Forward Gear

Forward gear, obviously, is used to move the boat ahead. It also plays a major role in "spinning" the vessel, which is the most efficient way to turn the boat.

Reverse Gear

Reverse gear is used to move the boat in a backwards motion. It also plays a major role in "spinning" the vessel, which is the most efficient way to turn the boat.

Neutral Gear

Neutral gear is engaged to slow the vessel, which is most desirable during docking. The momentum associated with neutral on these vessels is minimum. Usually, they must be in forward or reverse gear to move.

OUTBOARD, I/O, STERN-DRIVE

Steering Wheel

The steering wheel is used to change direction in forward or reverse gear. The response is immediate, since the position of the engine acts in unison with the wheel, directing the vessel to the desired location. Since no rudder is involved, the boat is directed as easily in reverse as it is in forward gear.

Throttle

The throttle is only used to overcome wind or current. Apply the throttle sparingly, since it tends to grow in intensity if overused. First we move quickly to port, then we must overact to starboard, etc.

OUTBOARD, I/O, STERN-DRIVE

Weight Distribution

In small vessels, weight distribution can have a direct effect on boat docking. Boats with weight toward the bow turn sooner in forward gear than boats with weight toward the stern. Conversely, boats with weight toward the stern turn sooner in reverse gear than boats with weight toward the bow. Boats with more weight on port side will turn more easily to port & vice-versa.

For example, when backing as in graphic below, it would be advantageous to have more weight in stern for earlier turn and more weight on port side for sharper turn to port.

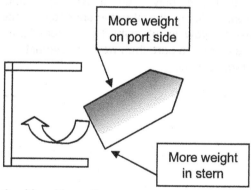

More weight on port side

More weight in stern

"Spinning Your Vessel"

"Spinning" your vessel is the primary means of docking and undocking successfully. It requires quick changes in wheel position and gears, but need not be done with throttle, unless there is strong wind/current to overcome.

OUTBOARD, I/O, STERN-DRIVE

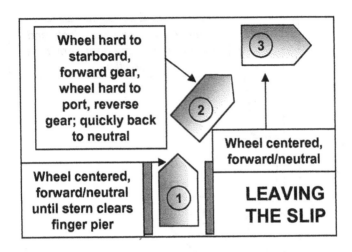

Wheel hard to starboard, forward gear, wheel hard to port, reverse gear; quickly back to neutral

Wheel centered, forward/neutral until stern clears finger pier

Wheel centered, forward/neutral

LEAVING THE SLIP

"SPINNING"

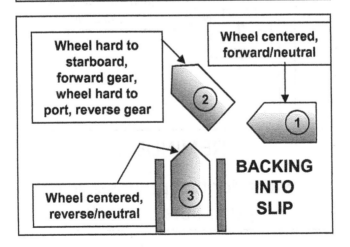

Wheel hard to starboard, forward gear, wheel hard to port, reverse gear

Wheel centered, forward/neutral

Wheel centered, reverse/neutral

BACKING INTO SLIP

OUTBOARD, I/O, STERN-DRIVE

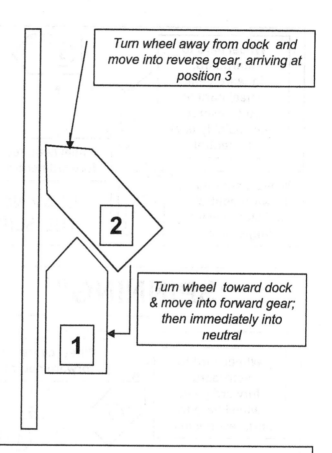

Turn wheel away from dock and move into reverse gear, arriving at position 3

2

Turn wheel toward dock & move into forward gear; then immediately into neutral

1

REMINDER:

watch for fuel pumps and/or pumpouts on dock

OUTBOARD, I/O, STERN-DRIVE

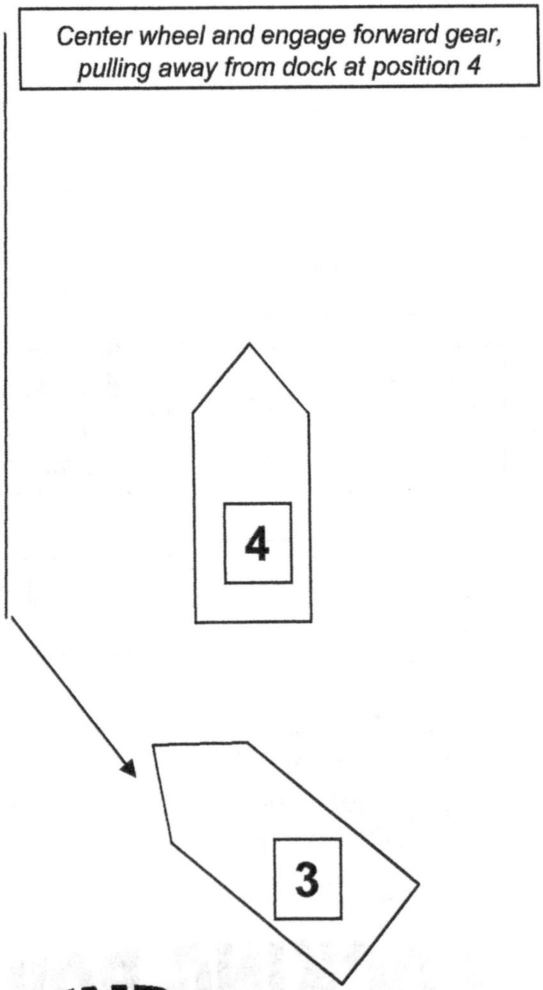

Center wheel and engage forward gear,
pulling away from dock at position 4

4

3

UNDOCKING

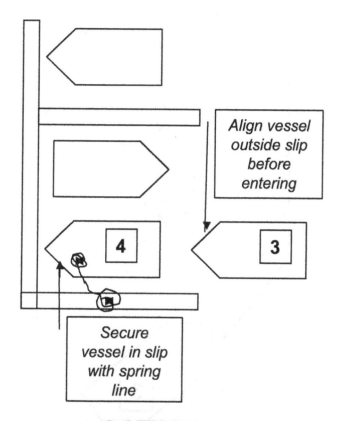

Align vessel outside slip before entering

4

3

Secure vessel in slip with spring line

DOCKING BOW-IN

OUTBOARD, I/O, STERN-DRIVE

Place fenders on both sides of vessel; turn wheel to starboard when stern of vessel aligns with final position in slip*; engage forward gear; back to neutral

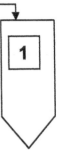

Stern of vessel is in alignment

2

Turn wheel hard to starboard; engage forward gear; wheel hard to port; engage reverse gear, spinning vessel into position 3

*Look for reference point on shore

CALM CONDITIONS

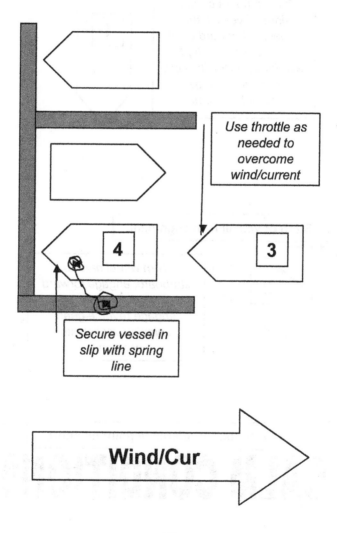

Use throttle as needed to overcome wind/current

4

3

Secure vessel in slip with spring line

Wind/Cur

OUTBOARD, I/O, STERN-DRIVE

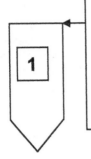

1

Place fenders on both sides of vessel; begin approach closer to slip since wind will drive boat away from it; do not allow wind to push the bow; turn wheel to starboard when stern of vessel aligns with final position in slip*; engage forward gear; back to neutral

Stern of vessel is in alignment

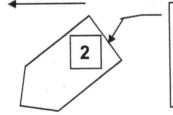

2

Turn wheel hard to starboard; engage forward gear; wheel hard to port; engage reverse gear, spinning vessel into position 3

*Look for reference point on shore

91

OUTBOARD, I/O, STERN-DRIVE

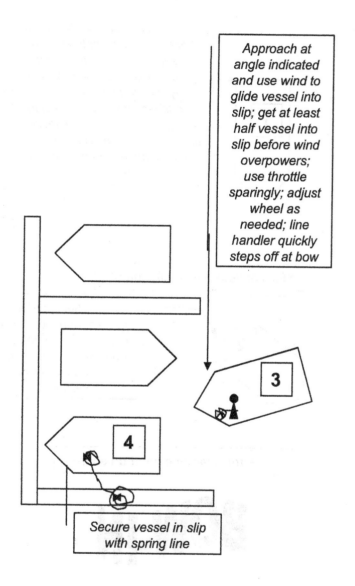

Approach at angle indicated and use wind to glide vessel into slip; get at least half vessel into slip before wind overpowers; use throttle sparingly; adjust wheel as needed; line handler quickly steps off at bow

3

4

Secure vessel in slip with spring line

OUTBOARD, I/O, STERN-DRIVE

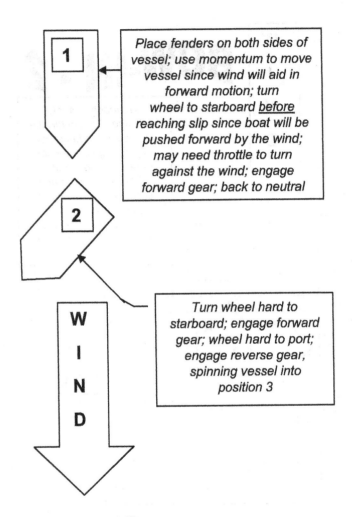

1

Place fenders on both sides of vessel; use momentum to move vessel since wind will aid in forward motion; turn wheel to starboard <u>before</u> reaching slip since boat will be pushed forward by the wind; may need throttle to turn against the wind; engage forward gear; back to neutral

2

Turn wheel hard to starboard; engage forward gear; wheel hard to port; engage reverse gear, spinning vessel into position 3

W
I
N
D

BOW-IN-1

OUTBOARD, I/O, STERN-DRIVE

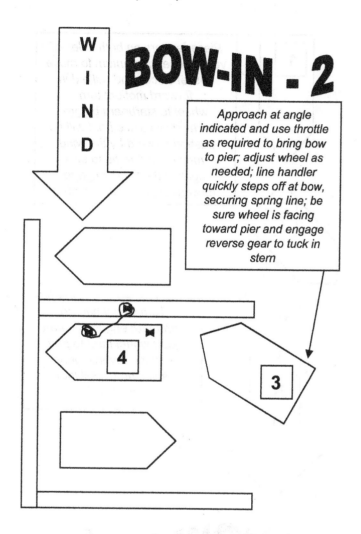

WIND

BOW-IN - 2

Approach at angle indicated and use throttle as required to bring bow to pier; adjust wheel as needed; line handler quickly steps off at bow, securing spring line; be sure wheel is facing toward pier and engage reverse gear to tuck in stern

4

3

OUTBOARD, I/O, STERN-DRIVE

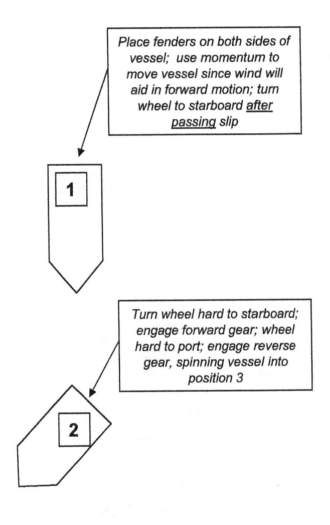

Place fenders on both sides of vessel; use momentum to move vessel since wind will aid in forward motion; turn wheel to starboard *after passing* slip

1

Turn wheel hard to starboard; engage forward gear; wheel hard to port; engage reverse gear, spinning vessel into position 3

2

OUTBOARD, I/O, STERN-DRIVE

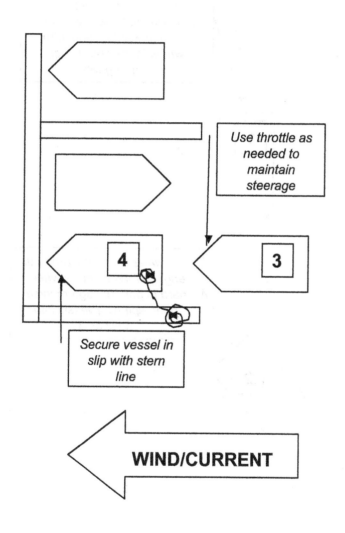

Use throttle as needed to maintain steerage

4

3

Secure vessel in slip with stern line

WIND/CURRENT

OUTBOARD, I/O, STERN-DRIVE

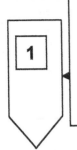

1 *Place fenders on both sides of vessel; begin approach further from slip since wind will drive boat towards it; do not allow wind to push the bow; turn wheel to starboard when stern of vessel aligns with final position in slip*; engage forward gear; back to neutral*

Stern of vessel is in alignment

2 *Turn wheel hard to starboard; engage forward gear; wheel hard to port; engage reverse gear, spinning vessel into position 3*

*Look for reference point on shore

BOW-IN

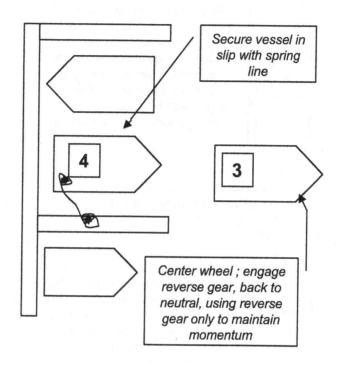

Secure vessel in slip with spring line

Center wheel ; engage reverse gear, back to neutral, using reverse gear only to maintain momentum

DOCKING STERN-IN

OUTBOARD, I/O, STERN-DRIVE

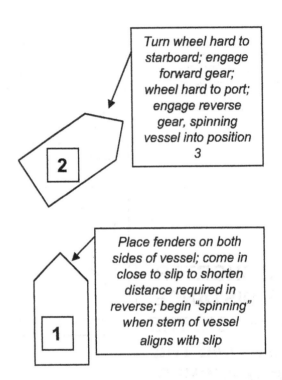

2 — Turn wheel hard to starboard; engage forward gear; wheel hard to port; engage reverse gear, spinning vessel into position 3

1 — Place fenders on both sides of vessel; come in close to slip to shorten distance required in reverse; begin "spinning" when stern of vessel aligns with slip

CALM CONDITIONS

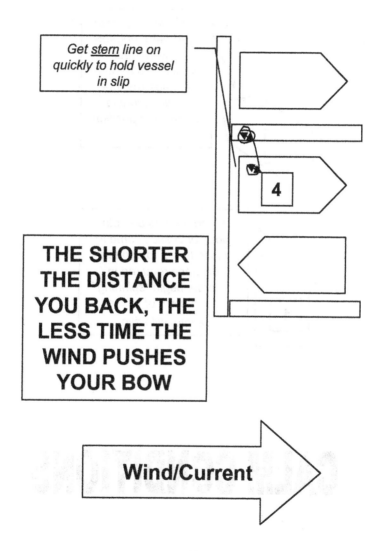

Get _stern_ line on quickly to hold vessel in slip

4

THE SHORTER THE DISTANCE YOU BACK, THE LESS TIME THE WIND PUSHES YOUR BOW

Wind/Current

OUTBOARD, I/O, STERN-DRIVE

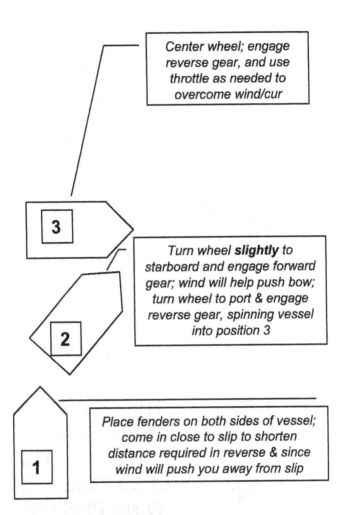

Center wheel; engage reverse gear, and use throttle as needed to overcome wind/cur

3

Turn wheel **slightly** to starboard and engage forward gear; wind will help push bow; turn wheel to port & engage reverse gear, spinning vessel into position 3

2

1

Place fenders on both sides of vessel; come in close to slip to shorten distance required in reverse & since wind will push you away from slip

STERN-IN

OUTBOARD, I/O, STERN-DRIVE

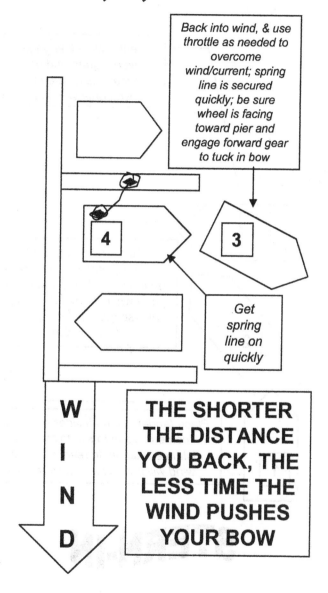

Back into wind, & use throttle as needed to overcome wind/current; spring line is secured quickly; be sure wheel is facing toward pier and engage forward gear to tuck in bow

4

3

.Get spring line on quickly

**W
I
N
D**

THE SHORTER THE DISTANCE YOU BACK, THE LESS TIME THE WIND PUSHES YOUR BOW

OUTBOARD, I/O, STERN-DRIVE

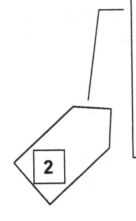

Let bow pass slip before beginning turn; turn wheel slightly to starboard; wind will whip bow quickly to starboard so immediately turn wheel to port and engage reverse gear, 'spinning" vessel into angle of position 3

Place fenders on both sides of vessel; come in close to slip to shorten distance required in reverse; engage forward gear & back to neutral; do not allow wind to catch the bow

STERN-IN

OUTBOARD, I/O, STERN-DRIVE

OUTBOARD, I/O, STERN-DRIVE, SINGLE-ENGINE VESSELS!

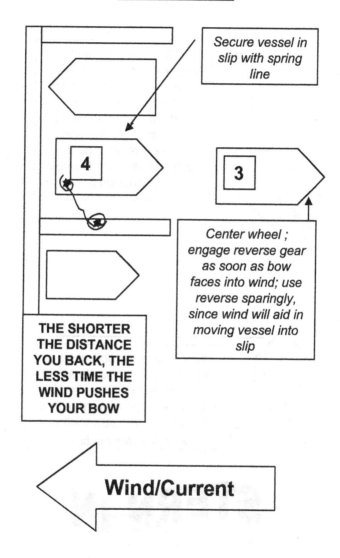

Secure vessel in slip with spring line

4

3

Center wheel ; engage reverse gear as soon as bow faces into wind; use reverse sparingly, since wind will aid in moving vessel into slip

THE SHORTER THE DISTANCE YOU BACK, THE LESS TIME THE WIND PUSHES YOUR BOW

Wind/Current

OUTBOARD, I/O, STERN-DRIVE

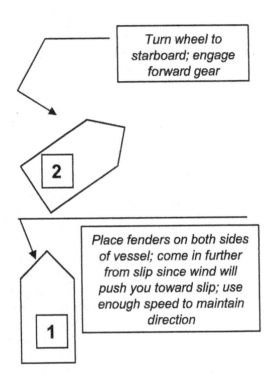

Turn wheel to starboard; engage forward gear

2

Place fenders on both sides of vessel; come in further from slip since wind will push you toward slip; use enough speed to maintain direction

1

STERN-IN

OUTBOARD, I/O, STERN-DRIVE

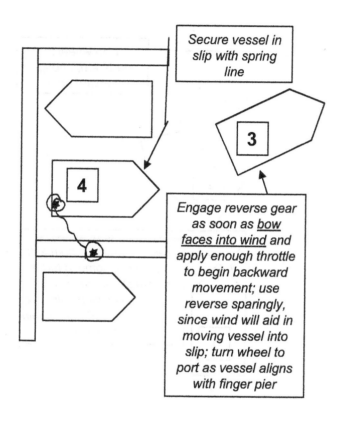

Secure vessel in slip with spring line

3

4

Engage reverse gear as soon as <u>bow faces into wind</u> and apply enough throttle to begin backward movement; use reverse sparingly, since wind will aid in moving vessel into slip; turn wheel to port as vessel aligns with finger pier

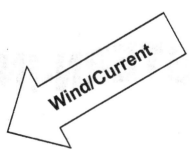

Wind/Current

OUTBOARD, I/O, STERN-DRIVE

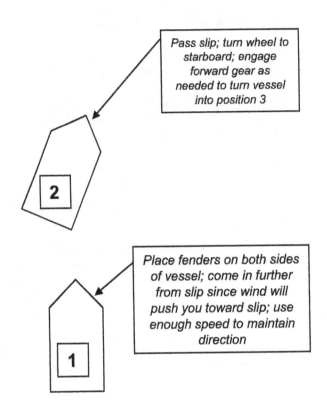

Pass slip; turn wheel to starboard; engage forward gear as needed to turn vessel into position 3

2

Place fenders on both sides of vessel; come in further from slip since wind will push you toward slip; use enough speed to maintain direction

1

STERN-IN

OUTBOARD, I/O, STERN-DRIVE

SKILL DRILLS

Build the muscles of successful boat docking by practicing the following on the water:

Get close enough to any object so you can judge boat movement, but not close enough to hit.

Stage 1: *Concentration on development of boat control skills in calm conditions, no wind/current. Use gear shift & steering wheel only; no throttle.*

Start and stop in forward gear, with steering wheel centered [using reverse to stop]

Start and stop in reverse gear, with steering wheel centered [using forward to stop]

Align bow with stationary object; steering wheel centered; start in forward gear and return to neutral; let momentum continue to move boat forward until steerage is lost or vessel stops; hold vessel in same position

Align stern with stationary object; steering wheel centered; start in reverse gear and return to neutral; let momentum continue to move boat backwards until steerage is lost or vessel stops; hold vessel in same position

[Idle speed means no throttle, just going to forward or reverse gear. The following turns to port or starboard are begun by turning wheel in appropriate direction BEFORE engaging gear.]

Turn to port in forward gear at continuous idle speed [note arc]

OUTBOARD, I/O, STERN-DRIVE

SKILL DRILLS

Turn to port in forward gear at intermittent idle speed [forward/neutral, forward/neutral] [note arc]

Turn to starboard in forward gear at continuous idle speed [note arc]

Turn to starboard in forward gear at intermittent idle speed [forward/neutral, forward/neutral] [note arc]

Turn to port in reverse gear at continuous idle speed [note arc]

Turn to port in reverse gear at intermittent idle speed [reverse/neutral, reverse/neutral] [note arc]

Turn to starboard in reverse gear at continuous idle speed [note arc]

Turn to starboard in reverse gear at intermittent idle speed [reverse/neutral, reverse/neutral] [note arc]

Turn to port in forward gear at intermittent idle speed, then shift into reverse and note boat reaction

Turn to starboard in forward gear at intermittent idle speed, then shift into reverse and note boat reaction

Practice boat's turning circle to port in forward gear

Practice spinning vessel by turning wheel hard to port, forward gear, then quickly wheel hard to starboard, reverse gear

OUTBOARD, I/O, STERN-DRIVE

SKILL DRILLS

Practice boat's turning circle to starboard in forward gear

Practice spinning vessel by turning wheel hard to starboard, forward gear, then quickly wheel hard to port, reverse gear

Practice boat's turning circle to port in reverse gear

Practice spinning vessel by turning wheel hard to port, reverse gear, then quickly wheel hard to starboard, forward gear

Practice boat's turning circle to starboard in reverse gear

Practice spinning vessel by turning wheel hard to starboard, reverse gear, then quickly wheel hard to port, forward gear

Practice bringing boat to full stop with varying amounts of speed, including full speed

Practice all maneuvers again, but put vessel into neutral after each gear engagement and let boat's momentum move vessel until she begins to stop or lose steerage

OUTBOARD, I/O, STERN-DRIVE

SKILL DRILLS

Stage 2: *concentration on development of boat control skills with wind/current. Stage 2 skill development uses gear shift and throttle, as well as steering wheel.*

Practice stage 1 skill drills in open water with wind/current, applying throttle as needed to overcome the elements.

TWIN ENGINE

Vessels with inboard or outboard twin engines handle similarly. They have eleven components which play a role in the boat docking process.

Neutral Gear – Momentum Moving Vessel

Forward Gear – Port Engine Only

Forward Gear – Starboard Engine Only

Forward Gear – Both Engines

Reverse Gear – Port Engine Only

Reverse Gear – Starboard Engine Only

Reverse Gear – Both Engines

Forward Port – Reverse Starboard Engines

Forward Starboard – Reverse Port Engines

Steering Wheel

Throttles [Pre-Set or As Needed]

Neutral Gear – Momentum Moving Vessel

Ninety percent of the boat docking process is done in neutral, with momentum moving vessel to its destination. Neutral gear separates the pros from the neophytes. The only time the vessel is in any other gear is to keep the vessel moving, change the direction, or overcome wind/current.

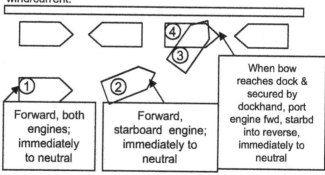

| ① Forward, both engines; immediately to neutral | ② Forward, starboard engine; immediately to neutral | When bow reaches dock & secured by dockhand, port engine fwd, starbd into reverse, immediately to neutral |

TWIN ENGINE

Gear Shifts

P=Port, S=Starboard

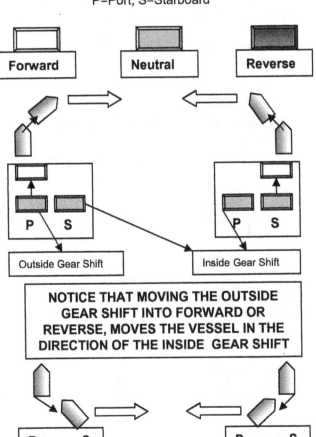

| Forward | Neutral | Reverse |

Outside Gear Shift

Inside Gear Shift

NOTICE THAT MOVING THE OUTSIDE GEAR SHIFT INTO FORWARD OR REVERSE, MOVES THE VESSEL IN THE DIRECTION OF THE INSIDE GEAR SHIFT

P S

P S

TWIN ENGINE

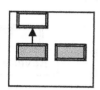

Forward Gear – Port Engine Only
To turn the boat to starboard, engage the port engine only into forward gear.

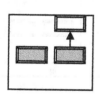

Forward Gear – Starboard Engine Only
To turn the boat to port, engage the starboard engine only into forward gear.

Forward Gear – Both Engines
To go straight ahead quickly, or when in open water and desiring to go straight ahead, engage both engines in forward gear. Be sure wheel is centered.

TWIN ENGINE

Reverse Gear – Port Engine Only
To back to starboard, engage the port engine only into reverse gear.

Reverse Gear – Starboard Engine Only
To back to port, engage the starboard engine only into reverse gear.

Reverse Gear – Both Engines
To back quickly, engage both engines in reverse gear.

TWIN ENGINE

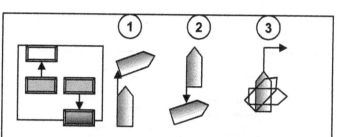

Forward Port, Reverse Starboard Engines

1. **With momentum moving forward**, to turn boat *sharply* to starboard, engage the port engine into forward gear and the starboard engine into reverse gear.

2. **With momentum moving backward**, to turn boat *sharply* to port in reverse, engage the port engine into forward gear and the starboard engine into reverse gear.

3. **With no momentum**, to turn boat in a circle toward starboard, engage the port engine into forward gear and the starboard engine into reverse gear.

Steering Wheel
Use of the steering wheel in docking with twin engines is contingent upon the vessel. It has been my experience that larger, heavier vessels hold their own against the elements, so that there is no need to use the steering wheel during docking; the gear shifts suffice. However, in smaller, lighter vessels, the steering wheel can play a vital role in the docking process. To be most effective in changing direction, the wheel should be turned in the appropriate direction BEFORE engaging gear.

TWIN ENGINE

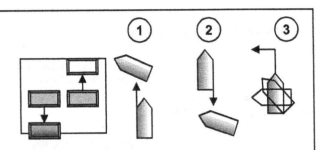

Forward Starboard, Reverse Port Engines

1. With momentum moving forward, to turn boat *sharply* to port, engage the starboard engine into forward gear and the port engine into reverse gear.

2. With momentum moving backward, to turn boat *sharply* to starboard in reverse, engage the starboard engine into forward gear and the port engine into reverse gear.

3. With no momentum, to turn boat in a circle toward port, engage the starboard engine into forward gear and the port engine into reverse gear.

TWIN ENGINE

Throttles [Pre-Set or As Needed]

Preset rpms may only be useful if your vessel has separate shifts for gear and throttle. If the gear and throttle are in the same handle, this component of docking is unavailable to you.

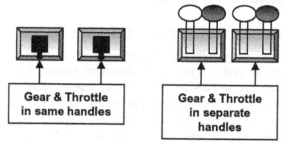

| Gear & Throttle in same handles | Gear & Throttle in separate handles |

The purpose of presetting rpms is to provide additional maneuvering power when docking your vessel. Before raising rpms, check your engine manual for the highest throttle rpms in which gears can be safely changed from forward to reverse without damaging the transmission.

What we are actually doing here is the equivalent of pressing your foot on the gas pedal of your car while in neutral, and before putting it in drive. This is extremely effective in handling twin-engine inboards, since the gear shifts alone may then manage to overcome wind and/or current, without having to use the throttles.

Set-up the preset rpms when the vessel is in neutral. Move the throttle shifts forward until the manufacturer's maximum level is reached. Then, use your gear shifts as needed to successfully dock your boat.

TWIN ENGINE

Throttles [Pre-Set or As Needed]

The throttle should only be used to overcome wind or current. Apply the throttle sparingly, since it tends to grow in intensity if overused. First we move quickly to port, then we must overact to starboard, etc.

The throttle can also be applied to one gear shift only, to correct an imbalance during the docking process. For example:

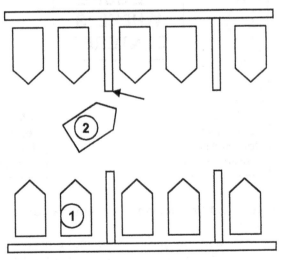

In the scenario above, the vessel is leaving the slip. The port engine is in forward gear and the starboard is in reverse. At position 2, the boat is getting too close to arrowed pier. By applying a little throttle to the starboard engine momentarily, which is in reverse, the boat can be redirected away from the pier, without having to adjust the gear shifts.

TWIN ENGINE

Moving Straight Along Dock or Pier

Twin-engine vessels can be moved forward or backward along a dock or pier with ease by placing the inside engine [the one closest to the dock or pier] in forward or reverse gear.

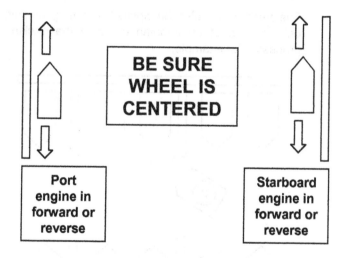

BE SURE WHEEL IS CENTERED

Port engine in forward or reverse

Starboard engine in forward or reverse

To review boat docking procedures for twin-engine vessels:

Use only gear shifts to dock & undock
Use wheel only if vessel does not respond sufficiently with shifts
Avoid using throttle, except in extreme conditions

TWIN ENGINE

There are numerous options that lead to successful docking and undocking with twin engines. Following are some suggestions.

TWIN ENGINE

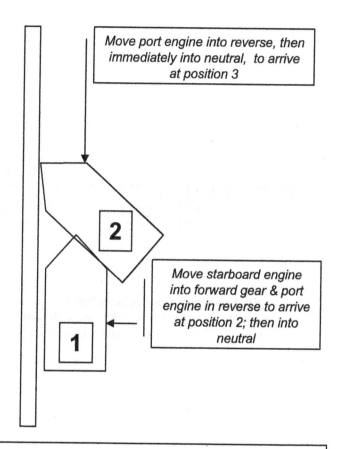

Move port engine into reverse, then immediately into neutral, to arrive at position 3

Move starboard engine into forward gear & port engine in reverse to arrive at position 2; then into neutral

REMINDER: watch for fuel pumps and/or pumpouts on dock

TWIN ENGINE

Place starboard engine into forward gear, leaving port engine in forward, and pull away

Move port engine into forward gear to arrive at position 4

4

3

UNDOCKING

TWIN ENGINE

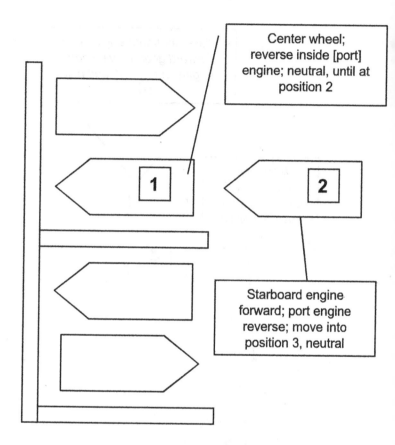

Center wheel; reverse inside [port] engine; neutral, until at position 2

1

2

Starboard engine forward; port engine reverse; move into position 3, neutral

LEAVING

TWIN ENGINE

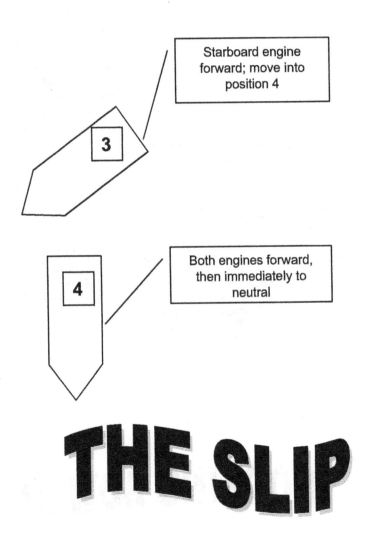

Starboard engine forward; move into position 4

Both engines forward, then immediately to neutral

THE SLIP

TWIN ENGINE

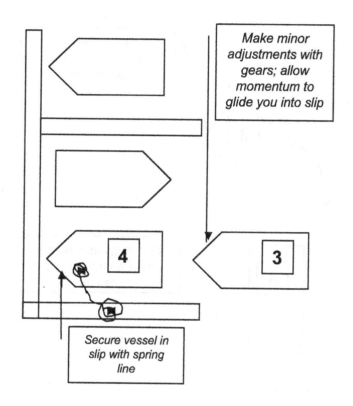

Make minor adjustments with gears; allow momentum to glide you into slip

4

3

Secure vessel in slip with spring line

DOCKING BOW-IN

TWIN ENGINE

Place fenders on both sides of vessel; engage forward gear with either the port or starboard engine, depending upon position; go back into neutral

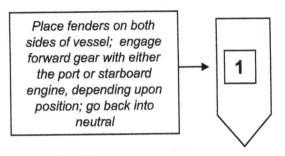

1

Stern of vessel is in alignment

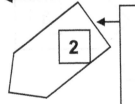

2

When stern aligns with slip*, place port engine in fwd, starboard engine in reverse, then back to neutral when reaching position 3

*Look for reference point on shore

CALM CONDITIONS

TWIN ENGINE

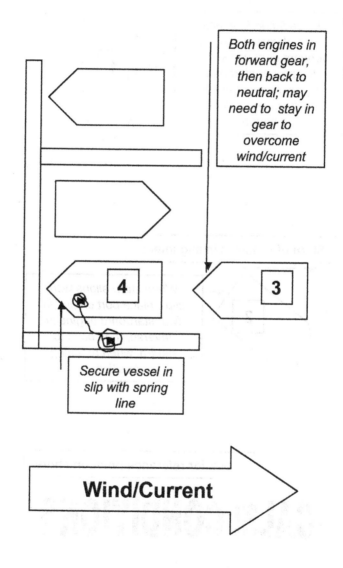

Both engines in forward gear, then back to neutral; may need to stay in gear to overcome wind/current

4

3

Secure vessel in slip with spring line

Wind/Current

TWIN ENGINE

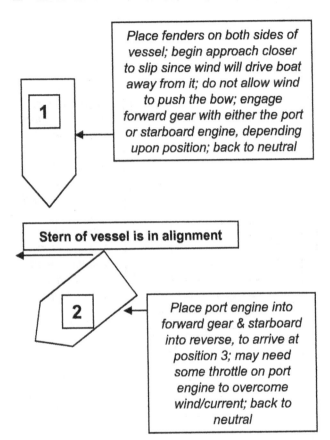

1

Place fenders on both sides of vessel; begin approach closer to slip since wind will drive boat away from it; do not allow wind to push the bow; engage forward gear with either the port or starboard engine, depending upon position; back to neutral

Stern of vessel is in alignment

2

Place port engine into forward gear & starboard into reverse, to arrive at position 3; may need some throttle on port engine to overcome wind/current; back to neutral

*Look for reference point on shore

BOW-IN

129

TWIN ENGINE

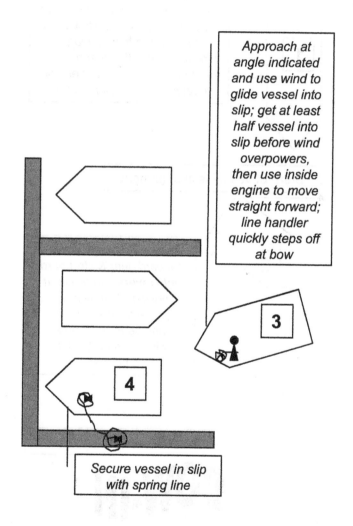

Approach at angle indicated and use wind to glide vessel into slip; get at least half vessel into slip before wind overpowers, then use inside engine to move straight forward; line handler quickly steps off at bow

3

4

Secure vessel in slip with spring line

TWIN ENGINE

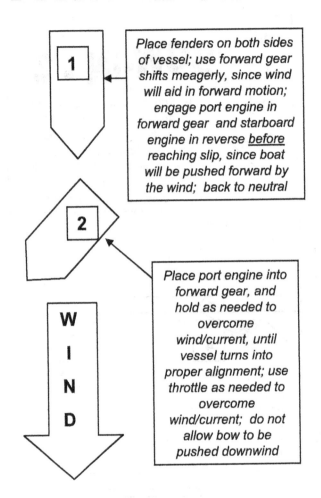

1 Place fenders on both sides of vessel; use forward gear shifts meagerly, since wind will aid in forward motion; engage port engine in forward gear and starboard engine in reverse <u>before</u> reaching slip, since boat will be pushed forward by the wind; back to neutral

2 Place port engine into forward gear, and hold as needed to overcome wind/current, until vessel turns into proper alignment; use throttle as needed to overcome wind/current; do not allow bow to be pushed downwind

WIND

BOW-IN-1

TWIN ENGINE

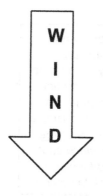

**W
I
N
D**

BOW-IN - 2

Approach at angle indicated
and use throttle as required
to bring bow to pier; quick
starboard forward/port
reverse straightens boat; line
handler quickly steps off at
bow, securing spring line

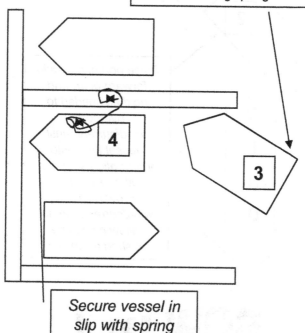

4

3

Secure vessel in
slip with spring
line

TWIN ENGINE

Place fenders on both sides of vessel; use forward gear shifts meagerly, since wind will aid in forward motion; engage port engine in forward gear and starboard engine in reverse after passing slip; back to neutral

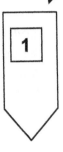

Place port engine into forward gear, and hold to overcome wind/current, until vessel turns into position 3; use starboard engine in reverse or throttle as needed to overcome wind/current; do not allow bow to be pushed downwind

TWIN ENGINE

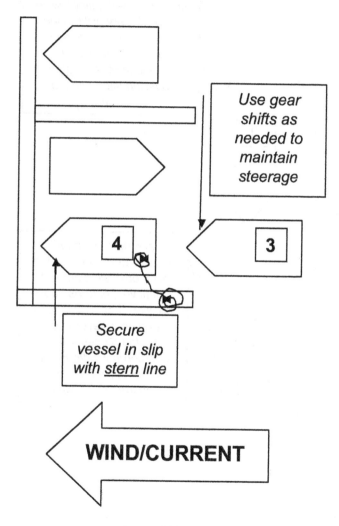

Use gear shifts as needed to maintain steerage

4

3

Secure vessel in slip with <u>stern</u> line

WIND/CURRENT

TWIN ENGINE

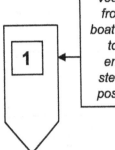

1

Place fenders on both sides of vessel; begin approach further from slip since wind will drive boat towards it; do not allow wind to push the bow; place port engine in forward gear when stern of vessel aligns with final position in slip*; back to neutral

Stern of vessel is in alignment

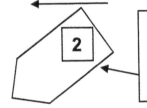

2

Use gear shifts sparingly in forward gear since wind/current will aid in driving boat to slip; move vessel into position 3

*Look for reference point on shore

BOW-IN

TWIN ENGINE

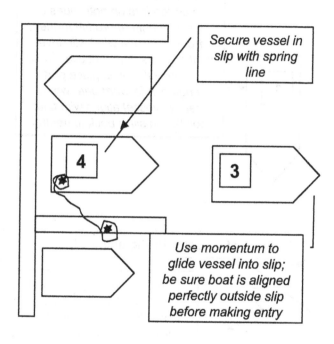

Secure vessel in slip with spring line

4

3

Use momentum to glide vessel into slip; be sure boat is aligned perfectly outside slip before making entry

DOCKING STERN-IN

TWIN ENGINE

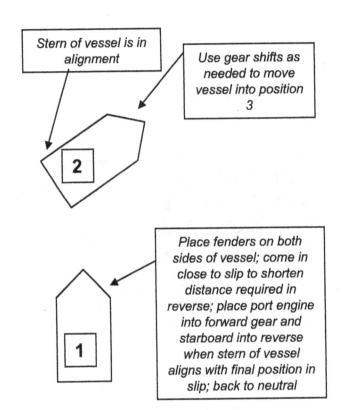

Stern of vessel is in alignment

Use gear shifts as needed to move vessel into position 3

2

Place fenders on both sides of vessel; come in close to slip to shorten distance required in reverse; place port engine into forward gear and starboard into reverse when stern of vessel aligns with final position in slip; back to neutral

1

CALM CONDITIONS

TWIN ENGINE

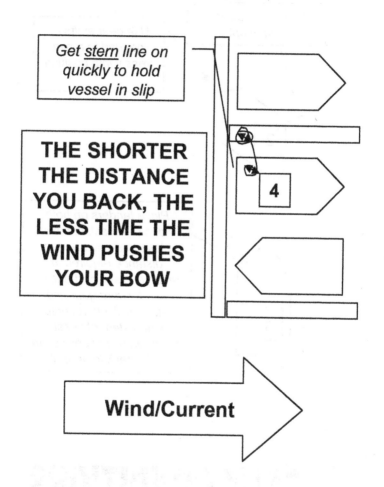

Get *stern* line on quickly to hold vessel in slip

THE SHORTER THE DISTANCE YOU BACK, THE LESS TIME THE WIND PUSHES YOUR BOW

4

Wind/Current

TWIN ENGINE

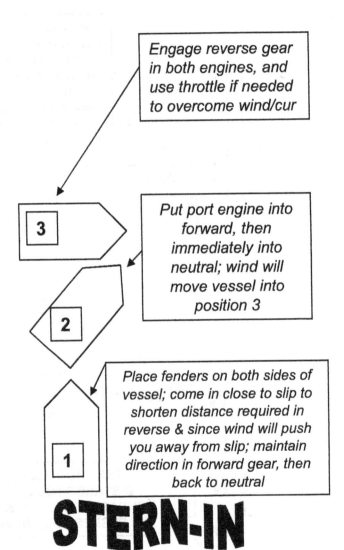

Engage reverse gear in both engines, and use throttle if needed to overcome wind/cur

3

Put port engine into forward, then immediately into neutral; wind will move vessel into position 3

2

Place fenders on both sides of vessel; come in close to slip to shorten distance required in reverse & since wind will push you away from slip; maintain direction in forward gear, then back to neutral

1

STERN-IN

TWIN ENGINE

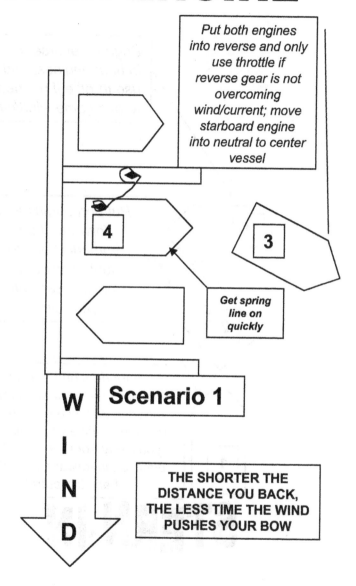

Put both engines into reverse and only use throttle if reverse gear is not overcoming wind/current; move starboard engine into neutral to center vessel

4

3

Get spring line on quickly

W
I
N
D

Scenario 1

THE SHORTER THE DISTANCE YOU BACK, THE LESS TIME THE WIND PUSHES YOUR BOW

TWIN ENGINE

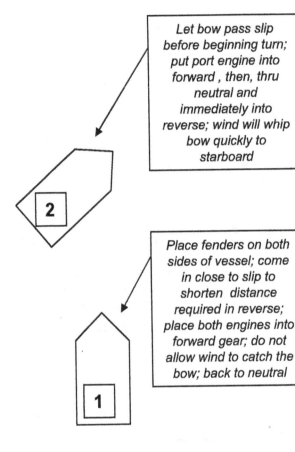

Let bow pass slip before beginning turn; put port engine into forward , then, thru neutral and immediately into reverse; wind will whip bow quickly to starboard

Place fenders on both sides of vessel; come in close to slip to shorten distance required in reverse; place both engines into forward gear; do not allow wind to catch the bow; back to neutral

STERN-IN

TWIN ENGINE

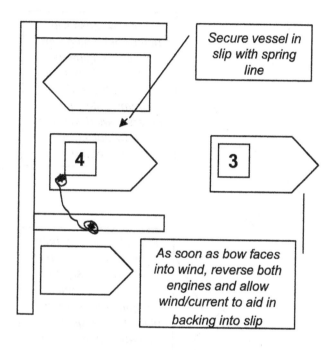

Secure vessel in slip with spring line

4

3

As soon as bow faces into wind, reverse both engines and allow wind/current to aid in backing into slip

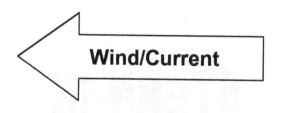

Wind/Current

TWIN ENGINE

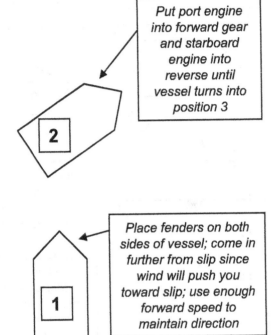

Put port engine into forward gear and starboard engine into reverse until vessel turns into position 3

2

Place fenders on both sides of vessel; come in further from slip since wind will push you toward slip; use enough forward speed to maintain direction

1

STERN-IN

TWIN ENGINE

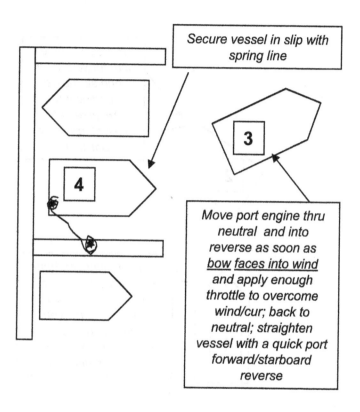

Secure vessel in slip with spring line

3

Move port engine thru
neutral and into
reverse as soon as
bow faces into wind
and apply enough
throttle to overcome
wind/cur; back to
neutral; straighten
vessel with a quick port
forward/starboard
reverse

4

Wind/Current

TWIN ENGINE

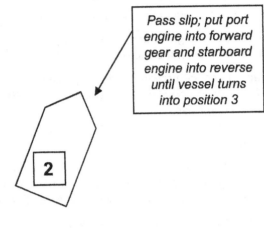

Pass slip; put port engine into forward gear and starboard engine into reverse until vessel turns into position 3

Place fenders on both sides of vessel; come in further from slip since wind will push you toward slip; use enough speed to maintain direction

STERN-IN

TWIN ENGINE

SKILL DRILLS

Build the muscles of successful boat docking by
practicing the following on the water:

*Get close enough to any object so you can judge boat
movement, but not close enough to hit:*

Stage 1: *concentration on development of boat control
skills in calm conditions, no wind/current. Stage 1 skill
development uses only gear shifts for steering; steering
wheel is centered for the entire exercise and no throttle
is applied.*

Start forward movement by moving both shifters into
forward gear; move shifters back to neutral and allow
momentum to move boat until steerage is affected

Start forward movement by moving both shifters into
forward gear; move shifters through neutral into reverse
to stop momentum; move shifters into neutral

Start backwards movement by moving both shifters into
reverse gear; move shifters back to neutral and allow
momentum to move boat until steerage is affected.

Start backwards movement by moving both shifters into
reverse gear; move shifters through neutral into forward
to stop momentum; move shifters into neutral

Move starboard shifter forward to begin turn to port; slip
port shifter into reverse; move starboard shifter into
neutral, keeping port shifter in reverse; place port shifter
into neutral

Move port shifter forward to begin turn to starboard; slip
starboard shifter into reverse; move port shifter into
neutral, keeping starboard shifter in reverse; place
starboard shifter into neutral

TWIN ENGINE

SKILL DRILLS

Move starboard shifter into reverse to begin stern turn to port; slip port shifter into forward; move both shifters into neutral

Move port shifter into reverse to begin stern turn to starboard; slip starboard shifter into forward; move both shifters into neutral

Move starboard shifter forward to begin turn to port; slip port shifter into reverse and hold until boat turns 90°; slip starboard shifter through neutral into reverse while moving port shifter into forward and hold until boat straightens

Move port shifter forward to begin turn to starboard; slip starboard shifter into reverse and hold until boat turns 90°; slip port shifter through neutral into reverse while moving starboard shifter forward and hold until boat straightens

Move starboard shifter into reverse to begin stern turn to port; slip port shifter into forward and hold until boat turns 90°; slip port shifter through neutral into reverse while moving starboard shifter into forward and hold until boat straightens

Move port shifter into reverse to begin stern turn to starboard; slip starboard shifter into forward and hold until boat turns 90°; slip starboard shifter through neutral into reverse while moving port shifter into forward and hold until boat straightens

Practice boat's forward turning circle to starboard by moving just port shifter forward, then into neutral, observing momentum to starboard

TWIN ENGINE

SKILL DRILLS

Practice boat's forward turning circle to starboard by moving port shifter forward and starboard shifter in reverse, then both shifters to neutral, observing momentum to starboard

Practice boat's forward turning circle to starboard by moving port shifter forward, port shifter neutral, starboard shifter reverse and hold until boat loses forward steerage, then into neutral

Practice boat's forward turning circle to starboard by combining all three steering options for fine-tuned steering; only port shifter forward; port shifter forward & starboard shifter in reverse; only starboard shifter in reverse

Practice boat's forward turning circle to port by moving just starboard shifter forward, then into neutral, observing momentum to port

Practice boat's forward turning circle to port by moving starboard shifter forward and port shifter in reverse, then both shifters to neutral, observing momentum to port

Practice boat's forward turning circle to port by moving starboard shifter forward, starboard shifter neutral, port shifter reverse and hold until boat loses forward steerage, then into neutral

Practice boat's forward turning circle to port by combining all three steering options for fine-tuned steering: only starboard shifter forward; starboard shifter forward & port shifter in reverse; only port shifter in reverse

TWIN ENGINE

SKILL DRILLS

Practice boat's backwards turning circle to starboard by moving just port shifter into reverse, then into neutral, observing momentum to starboard

Practice boat's backwards turning circle to starboard by moving port shifter into reverse and starboard shifter into forward, then both shifters into neutral, observing momentum to starboard

Practice boat's backwards turning circle to starboard by moving port shifter into reverse, port shifter neutral, starboard shifter forward and hold until boat loses reverse steerage, then into neutral

Practice boat's backwards turning circle to starboard by combining all three steering options for fine-tuned steering: only port shifter in reverse; port shifter in reverse & starboard shifter forward; only starboard shifter in forward

Practice boat's backwards turning circle to port by moving just starboard shifter to reverse, then into neutral, observing momentum to port

Practice boat's backwards turning circle to port by moving starboard shifter to reverse and port shifter forward, then both shifters to neutral, observing momentum to port

Practice boat's backwards turning circle to port by moving starboard shifter to reverse, starboard shifter neutral, port shifter forward and hold until boat loses backwards steerage, then into neutral

TWIN ENGINE

SKILL DRILLS

Practice boat's backwards turning circle to port by combining all three steering options for fine-tuned steering: only starboard shifter in reverse; starboard shifter in reverse & port shifter forward; only port shifter forward

Stage 2: *concentration on development of boat control skills with wind/current. Stage 2 skill development uses gear shift and throttle for steering; wheel is centered for the entire exercise.*

If gear shift and throttle are in one handle, throttle is applied by additional movement forward or reverse. Use only enough throttle to overcome effects of wind/current.

Practice the Stage 1 skill drills, applying throttle after each gear shift change.

If gear shift and throttle are in separate handles, see section on twin-engines, preset rpms.

Steering Wheel may be required in smaller, lighter vessels.

Practice the Stage 1 skill drills, applying appropriate steering wheel direction BEFORE each gear shift change.

DOCKING TECHNIQUES WITH PILINGS!

While the docking situations outlined in the previous sections apply to docking where pilings exist, there are a few specific situations where pilings can be particularly advantageous. For example:

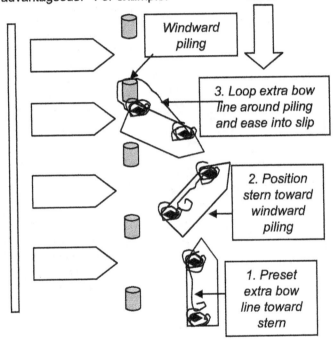

WIND

Windward piling

3. Loop extra bow line around piling and ease into slip

2. Position stern toward windward piling

1. Preset extra bow line toward stern

PILINGS

Another example: **WIND**

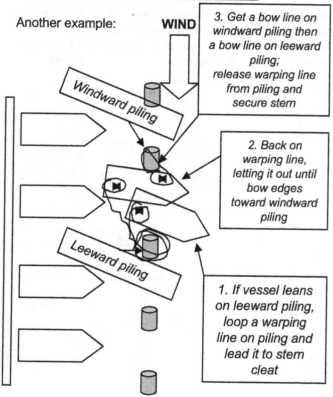

3. Get a bow line on windward piling then a bow line on leeward piling; release warping line from piling and secure stern

2. Back on warping line, letting it out until bow edges toward windward piling

1. If vessel leans on leeward piling, loop a warping line on piling and lead it to stern cleat

Windward piling

Leeward piling

BOW THRUSTER

BOW THRUSTER!!

Hydraulic: always available for use

Electric: available in short bursts

As long-time boaters, and boat dockers, we feel sure that divine intervention was involved in its creation and application. The Bow Thruster [notice that we capitalized it!] does what no other component of docking can do: IT MOVES THE BOAT SIDEWAYS WITHOUT FORWARD OR BACKWARD MOVEMENT.

BOW THRUSTER

BOW THRUSTER and why we love it!

Below is a graphic describing our experience at a fuel dock in Tortola, BVI. The Dockmaster asked us to bring the boat to the fuel dock for diesel fillup, starboard-side to, so we did not have to redo the fenders. When we arrived at position 5, we could not tuck in the bow without moving forward into the dock. The Bow Thruster did the job perfectly.

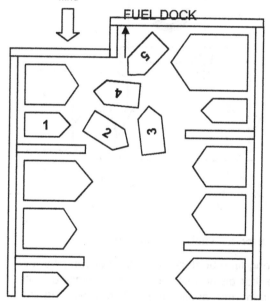

The vessel we were moving had twin engines, but the Bow Thruster was still a tool that changed a boat-bumping, line-stressing, situation into a no-brainer.

BOW THRUSTER

BOW THRUSTER!!

Many purists would disagree with us on this, but we think that anyone who could afford a Bow Thruster should get one. And while we have no personal experience with stern thrusters, ditto for them! To us, boating is about being on the water, enjoying its amazing pleasures and treasures, and any tool that makes docking easier is a good thing.

However, we do not want to mislead you into thinking that because you have a Bow Thruster you do not need to learn the basics of boat docking. A Bow Thruster is an amazing luxury that can help you out of tight situations, but does not replace the basic skills necessary to dock successfully.

While a Bow Thruster could be considered a luxury on a twin-engine or outboard/I/O/stern-drive vessel, it may be a necessity on single-engine inboards. Many of these vessels are difficult to steer in reverse and a Bow Thruster may overcome this weakness. For example:

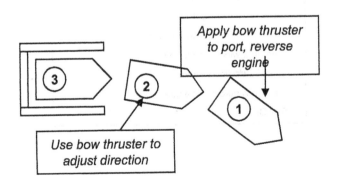

Apply bow thruster to port, reverse engine

Use bow thruster to adjust direction

INDEX OF VARIOUS
BOAT TYPES

INDEX OF VARIOUS
BOAT TYPES

INDEX OF VARIOUS BOAT TYPES